Into Thy Word Ministries
Presents

All about Small Groups!

How to Start and Lead Small Groups in your Church with His Power and Purpose!

Richard J. Krejcir

Dedication

-->

I dedicate this work to the GLORY OF OUR LORD!

To our God and Father be glory for ever and ever. Amen. Philippians 4:20

Many thanks to all the people who have discipled and inspired me over the years, such as Robert B. Munger, Chuck Miller, R.C. Sproul, and of course, my friend and mentor, Francis A. Schaeffer. A special thanks to my editors, who have worked very hard on the manuscript, and the people in my small group and Bible Study who have encouraged, prayed, given me insights, and kept me sane on this journey.

And, of course, my utmost dedication is to my great love with appreciation for all of her help—my wife, Mary Ruth. *"I found the one my heart loves"* Song of Solomon 3:4

For Christ's love compels us, because we are convinced that one died for all, and therefore all died. And he died for all, that those who live should no longer live for themselves but for him who died for them and was raised again. 2 Corinthians 5:14-15

Richard J. Krejcir

Contents

We are therefore Christ's ambassadors, as though God were making his appeal through us. We implore you on Christ's behalf: Be reconciled to God. 2 Corinthians 5:20

Devote yourselves to prayer, being watchful and thankful. And pray for us, too, that God may open a door for our message, so that we may proclaim the mystery of Christ, for which I am in chains. Pray that I may proclaim it clearly, as I should. Be wise in the way you act toward outsiders; make the most of every opportunity. Let your conversation be always full of grace, seasoned with salt, so that you may know how to answer everyone. Colossians 4:2-6

Preface

Why should I be in a Small Group?

Day after day, in the temple courts and from house to house, they never stopped teaching and proclaiming the good news that Jesus is the Messiah. Acts 5:42

This work is a deduction of over thirty years of research and experience to build effectual small group discipleship in the local church for God's Glory.

In Acts, the Bible tells us we need to be in relationships for our personal and spiritual growth. As Paul and the early Christians taught and received teaching *"from house to house,"* we also must respond in our walk with Christ in each others' homes (Acts 5:42; 20:20)! Even in the shadow of the Temple; they did this; even in the shadow of your Church, you can do this. Why did they do this? They needed connection with one another in their fragmented and persecuted world; we desperately need to be connected, too! They needed a way and place to do as Christ modeled and taught them--multiplying disciples, leaders, and churches so that God's Kingdom will be built and glorified.

Are you thinking, "This is great, but not for me"? Perhaps you are like me, struggling with a very full plate--a plate overflowing with things that you need to do and are responsible for in your life. We all struggle with the demands of careers—the frustrations and stresses placed on us, including goals, deadlines, work flow, and office politics.   Our family obligations are important; many of us have children who need us. Maybe you are already volunteering in the church or community. Perhaps you are juggling work, school, and family to the point that there is not a free minute. When you are asked, "Why don't you join our small group?", your reply may be, "What?! I do not have the time! I cannot possibly commit to anything else. I am overloaded and overwhelmed!" To be honest, you are the person who needs to be in a small group the most!

Why? It is God's plan for you to be in quality relationships to Him and with to others in the confines of a loving community-- the definition of "church." We all need a place to belong and work through the issues of life. We need to be loved and give our love. As Christians, our primary thrust is to know and grow in Christ, surrendering and giving to Christ's glory (John 14-15; Gal. 2:20-21; Phil. 3:10). How can this be accomplished when all aspects of our life are riddled with stress? With small group study, learning spiritual discipline and receiving the discipleship, relationships, and encouragement that small groups offer. We need a place to grow and we as humans in relationship to Christ grow best in community with people who love and care for you!

Why? We are called to be Fruitful. This is a call to be obedient, to multiply the seed given to us. We are to make disciples of His Word. We are to point to Christ, never to ourselves!

We need to be disciples of Christ, not of people like ourselves! This is a standard call of God to do something productive and effectual with our life and faith. To have this wondrous gift of salvation and do nothing with it is a great insult to our gift Giver, God; it is a proof of ingratitude and nonuse, which would prove that one is either not saved or highly disobedient and foolish (Isa. 27:6; Hos. 14:4-8; John 15).

Why? We are called to *bear fruit*, referring to a growing faith that is fed and focused on our response to Christ that motivates the Fruit of the Spirit and moral and virtuous thinking and action because of God's love to us and our gratitude and love back to Him. This is God's love and work in us that flows in through His Holy Spirit and out of us to others around us because we have a personal relationship with Christ. We have God's living presence in us, living in us (Matt. 6:10; John 15; Rom. 5:1-5; 12:1-21; 1 Cor. 12:1-14:40; Gal. 5:16-26; Eph. 4:1-6:20; 2 Peter 1:3-9).

What does it take to be a faithful and fruitful Christian, to be attached to Christ as His love and work flows in and through us? If we claim to know Christ as Lord and hang in His Church, we must yearn to imitate Him and follow His precepts, especially when we lead others! This happens when we show the faith to permanently leave our sinful lives—and, with overwhelming gratitude--follow Jesus. Small groups are the prime platforms for us to learn, grow, and to share. We must follow before we can lead. We are never to be isolated from one another as this will lead us to be unfaithful, prideful, manipulative, or abusive to the people God gives us to care for; such acts are wicked, and we will be held to a strict accounting (Jer. 23:1-2; 31:34; Ezek. 34:11-31; Mic. 5:4; 6:8; Hos. 6:6; John 15 and16; 17:21-23).

> *Small groups will help us produce faithfulness, which comes when we are in a state of right being; this can only come about from a right, growing relationship with God; this comes by accepting what Christ has done for us and applying it to our lives--by faith.*

This helps us create an atmosphere of happiness, contentment, and cooperation--the closest we get to living in real unity. It can only be grasped if/when we surrender our pride and sin and really live by what Christ has called us to. In my many years of helping people in their hurt or in recovery to transformation and effective ministry, we have all had to rely on the Vine. We need one another's experiences, giftedness, insights all rooted in the Word, and we Christ to help us to these means that glorify our Lord. People only change when they realize that the pain and challenge of the change is less than the pain and work of staying where they are. The sap will flow ever so more (Gal. 5:22-23; 3 John 1:2-4)!

> *Our greatest purpose is to build relationships with Him and with others; when we ignore this, we fail in the most important aspects in life, including our relationship in Him!*

Here are additional things to ponder:

1. Small groups are the perfect places to understand and practice authentic relationships to feel as members of God's family.

2. Small groups are the perfect places to practice our call to be disciplined and make disciples.

3. Small groups are the perfect places for Spiritual growth to make His truth come to life in our lives (Matt. 28:18-20).

4. Small groups are the perfect places to understand the Bible and heartfelt prayer and put it into action.

5. Small groups are the perfect places to unwind, release your stress, and prioritize your life.

6. Small groups are the perfect places to have our needs met and dealt with and fulfill those burdens in others in a stable community. In this way, we can handle stress, crisis, changes, and the pressures of life.

7. Small groups are the perfect places to be in study of His Word and to be in prayer; we may do this individually, but we are also to do it in community.

8. Small groups are the perfect places to welcome your friends into the church and introduce them to Christ.

9. Small groups are the perfect places to develop our skills, leadership, and ministry so we can be better servants of our Lord.

10. Small groups are the perfect places to understand how to share Christ with loved ones and coworkers.

11. Small groups are the perfect places to deepen your understanding and practice of worship.

12. Small groups are the perfect places to put into practice the teaching you are receiving from your church, radio, web and your personal devotions. Remember, the phrase *"one another"* is used over 50 times in the New Testament to describe our relationship to other believers. Small groups are the perfect places to be with one another!

I am excited to be a part of a small group in my church and have been for over 20 years; small groups are part of the vision of my church. The main reason I have stayed with my "home" church--even as a pastor in other churches--is due to my relationships I have developed and experienced through the Bible studies and small groups! We will not get much out of church if we just come to the services--as good as they are; we must get involved, and small groups are the perfect places to do this! Your church needs you, and I believe you may need them, too. If you would like to host a group, lead a group, or just attend a group, please take the initiative and get yourself plugged in! If leading or hosting scares, you remember this: At *Into Thy Word*, we have excellent training and resources for you. No experience is necessary; we have curriculum that teaches itself. You just have to show up.

Therefore encourage one another and build each other up, just as in fact you are doing. 1 Thessalonians 5:11

Chapter 1

Getting to Know You!

As iron sharpens iron, so one man sharpens another.
Proverbs 27:17

Warning! The Spirit General has determined that Small Groups are detrimental to your complacency (self-satisfied versus Christ-satisfied)!

Proverbs 25:12; 27:17; Colossians 3:12-17; 1 Thessalonians 5:12-16

> *The Small Group is the prime platform for establishing and instilling the Great Commandment and the Great Commission that Jesus gave us in Matthew 28:18-20 and Mark 12:29-31.*

The Small Group is also the vehicle with which to develop and experience authentic relationships and growing discipleship. This builds a Church of authentic community, poured out to His precepts and being in relational intimacy and fullness in Him. This is what we are called to emulate from our Lord. Because people will be learning and growing, they will move from personal agendas and pride to growth and service to our Lord. This produces a supportive environment that has love, care,

1

hospitality, and the Spirit impacting the people. This fosters the engagement of the community and world for the Gospel.

Heed this warning! People may fight you; it will take work and effort, and at times, you may think of giving up--do not! He is with you, and He will empower you; you have to work for it, too! **You can do it!**

If you do not want to work or put forth the effort, if you just want a nice club--a place where the people can easily be manipulated and controlled--or if you want a place to rule and to spur on your personal power and yoke, do not have Small Groups in your church! Small Groups are where the Lord is at work, and you do not want Christ getting His Way in the way of your personal agenda and pride! Satire aside, for Small Groups to work, you must be willing and able to let Christ truly work in you personally and in your church collectively! This will conquer complacency and move us from being self-satisfied to being Christ-satisfied. Allowing Him to further conquer our fears and pride will enable us to move onward to spiritual maturity. Small Groups are the best vehicles to do this along with our personal Bible reading, devotions, and prayer time. Small Groups will take what we have learned in our quiet time, then add to it, hone it, sharpen it, pressure cook it, and release it into service and community.

Think about this point: How do we live the Christian life? How do we apply His precepts?

In First Corinthians 11:1, Paul tells us to *follow my example, as I follow the example of Christ*. We are called to be people who learn of His Word and impart that knowledge to others (Matt. 28:18-20; Acts 1:4-14). Most of us live in a culture that fosters isolation, personal pride, loneliness, individualistic mindsets, hedonism, suspicion, distrust, and the fear of being vulnerable. Thus, we have to put forth an effort to live the Christian life! In over 20 years of pastoral ministry, I have found no better way to take what we learn from the church and Word, work it out in our hearts and minds and make an application with it than in Small Groups! Small Groups are essential and necessary in building supportive and meaningful relationships and Bible learning; they must be a part of every church who seeks to know our Lord and make Him known. This helps create a church of real purpose—God's purpose—of dependence on God and the independence of one another. Without Small Groups, we will fall far short of learning and applying His precepts into our lives and community. We will have a church that is fragmented, disconnected, isolated, and meaningless!

So, why are there not more churches doing this? Is it just because it requires much work and there may be resentments and hesitations? Actually, because Small Groups can be scary, people will start to grow; and, those who are not growing, especially some pastors and church leaders, will become fearful and fight against them. These are the people who will give the most resistance! Personal agendas will be challenged and the godly life will transpire along with His purposes running the Church. This is what we are called to; however, our sinful nature gets in the way of His Way! Christ usually does not force Himself, so we continue in our pride when we could have had abundantly more in Him! Small Groups can also be dangerous as they denote alteration in the typical way people "do" their church, and may go against some traditions and mindsets that do not embrace change or conviction. The enemy to Small Groups is our complacency. Complacency is like pride; it hates being impacted by the Holy Spirit and detests the application of Scripture to Christian living. Small Groups will kick the complacency out. Make sure you want it out. You and your church cannot grow spiritually until you want to and are willing to put your effort into it (Acts. 2:46-47)! Small Groups are the way to grow your church in Him!

What is a Small Group?

The definition of a Small Group can vary for as many Small Groups as are out there. A Small Group characteristically is a group of committed people who come together on a regular basis for a specific function—that of the growth and discovery of God's precepts from His Word. The basic idea is a group of people, from three to twelve in number, who come together for connection in their faith building and fellowship. This can also include accountability, recovery, evangelistic, discipleship, and various other learning and personal need groups. The effective Small Group will always have an open Bible, have committed prayer, and the attitude of care for the people who are there! Small Groups can be the "rubber that meets the road" of the ministry of your church and community!

We all need to have encouragement, connection, advice, and support from a community of Believers who are growing in Him. It should be a place to reflect on our life and situation, build community, encourage accountability, study the Bible and learn to apply it, pray for others, and reach out to the world around us. *Learning to* do life together, receive care, discipleship, and learning, and learning about the ways of God through the Bible and prayer will build us up as individuals and as a church. Faith must inspire us before we can do outreach effectively (Matt. 4:18-19)! Small Groups are geared to provide all church members a rewarding benefit from their experiences in the church, and that benefit is their growth and maturity in Him that translates into character and to outreach as His witness!

How they benefit the Church

Do you have a church that is so big it is not meeting the needs of its members? Perhaps your church has magnificent worship and impacting teaching; that is why you came, but you feel disconnected. Perhaps you feel your church is too small and see no opportunities, or there is no good teaching there, but you feel you are cared for there. Maybe your church is too small because it is stagnating and that is why it is not growing. Is your church just right but something is missing? The answer is Small Groups. Small Groups answer the question, *How do I grow in Christ and grow my church?* We grow by growing in Him! Small Groups become the hub of learning, care, outreach, discipleship, and lead in nurturing, encouraging, and spiritual formation.

The Church needs to emphasize Small Groups as an essential primary ministry.

Why? Small Groups help fill you with His awe and wonder (Acts 2:42-47). Jesus Himself was in a Small Group of twelve. The Church got its start in Acts from Small Groups. This is how our Lord chose to model ministry personally and to launch His Church. The early church *devoted themselves* to Jesus' teaching and to one another. It was the Small Group where the Spirit impacted people and empowered them for ministry. It was the Small Groups where community and function were formed, even before the persecution came. The Lord blessed them and used them; we have no excuse not to do the same. The Church and your church must have Small Groups at its core--not a few here and there, but all encompassing for all stages of life and ministry, from youth to the elderly. If you want to grow your church in spiritual maturity (which is far more important than growing numerically, but usually creates numerical growth, too), Small Groups are the way; if you want to grow your church membership and worship, you must have spiritual maturity and a place to invite the people in--as Acts tells us, *He added to their number*!

The people in your church live in a disconnected and stress-filled world. Relationships are few and fragile and His Word is rarely applied. Without Small Groups, you cannot effectively grow your church or effectively or efficiently care for your people. Your church will not have depth, maturity, or much community impact without the caring, prayers, and support of its people. A pastor and/or staff cannot effectively meet the needs of all of the people. A pastor must train and equip others; this is what lay ministry is all about. Ministry and relationships form and accumulate best in Small Groups. When people are hurting, need direction, or can help others, it comes from the Small Group. Ministry and impacting the neighborhood comes from the Small Group. Your church will grow and be used by God through the Small Group. Small Groups are not to replace the church's worship and teaching; rather, they are the participants and conventioneers of the church. Consider a church a convention of Small Groups united for prayer, worship, instruction, the proclamation of His Word, and synergistic ministry. Your church is called to make Small Groups!

The Hurdles

The biggest reason why people do not join Small Groups is because they are fearful. Being vulnerable to people who may intentionally or unintentionally betray you is very scary. For some, it is scary to meet new people, go to a stranger's house, or take the time to make such a commitment. In addition, to share your life and woes with a stranger or to be afraid that you may not know the answers and look stupid in front of others is threatening. However, we have to get over our fears and embrace the community. We do not need to know the answers, but we are to be willing to discover them. When we share with others, we commune and grow tighter and together, building community and effectual relationships. Yes, people will hurt you, and you will hurt others. But, we still need one another; we need forgiveness, to be willing to forgive others, and to be open and vulnerable. This is a *must* to growing in faith. The main hurdle is YOU, and your willingness to more deeply pursue your faith and your relationships. We need one another to grow further in the faith!

> *To be successful in a Small Group, the participants need to know that we are created from community for community by a triune God. As Christians, we are called to know one another.*

Just look up "one another" in a concordance and see all of the passages listed. We are made for community; we need community. But, that does not mean it will just magically function. We all have to put in the effort and take the risks. Once you are willing to take the risks, then the time, commitment, and effort to press on will become easier as you see the benefits outweighing your fears. A good program, introducing Small Groups by easing people in them with testimonies and demonstration in a safe environment, will help alleviate these fears.

Types of Small Groups

Whether you call them home fellowship groups, home groups, Alpha Groups, Beta Groups, community groups, encounter groups, Lighthouses, Life Groups, Kinship groups, share groups, growth groups, His groups, home Bible studies or discipleship groups, they all are places to come together for learning, worship, prayer, encouragement, accountability, celebration, personal support, fellowship, and community building. There is no set formula, schedule, or singular purpose. A Small Group is a place to learn and grow and to equip and be equipped to glorify our Lord. It is a place to learn and build relationships. It is a place to know, understand, experience, and to share love and joy. It is a place to learn and develop character. It is a place to prepare and help prepare others for His service. However, it is my opinion that a Small Group without the Bible is just a club with no distinction or purpose and no real way to grow. A Small Group can use other books, articles, and curriculum, or just be a safe place to talk about your day; at some point, though, the Bible must be opened and His Word must be engaged. His redemptive plan must impact you! The bottom line is that a Small Group is a place to know Christ and one another (Acts 1:12-14; 2:1-4).

Small Groups have no set time, place, or duration. They can meet for periods of a few weeks to being permanent fellowships. I have seen groups last just a few sessions and they dissolve while others have been meeting for over thirty years regularly and consistently. They can meet weekly, bi-weekly, or monthly, although the more consistent you are, the more you will get out of it. Small Groups meet best in people's homes that are comfortable and inviting; this helps in learning and attitude and gives the opportunity to invite people who may not normally come to a church.

Small Groups have no set number of participants, although the optimal number is dependent on the personalities and goals of the participants. The numbers I have found to be best over the years is from four to 10, seven being the prime. For Jesus, it was 12 (Mark 3:13-14). A Small Group can range from three to twelve to hundreds of people. The big groups of over 20 to 2000, to be real Small Groups, meet corporately for worship and instruction, and then section themselves off into groups of five to 10 for deeper learning, prayer, and application. Small Groups timing can be any day or time when the participants are available. You can meet for an hour, an hour and a half, two hours, every week, every other week, or once a month. You can meet at church, an office, the library (get permission), at a coffee house, or restaurant. However, it is always best to meet at a home. You can just have fellowship and a topic study, or incorporate worship, Bible study, and outreach.

> *Who is supposed to be in the Small Groups? Pastors? Church leaders? Deacons? Elders? Only the spiritually mature? Only for new Christians? The answer is everyone!*

Everyone *who claims Jesus as Lord* should and must be in a Small Group or Bible study, and *people who do not know the Lord* should be in a Small Group, for that is the best way to continue and grow in the faith. It is a means to reach your full potential, growth, maturity, share the faith, and be better used by our Lord!

Some of the Main types of Small Groups (Ecclesiastes. 4:9; 4:12):

Two are better than one, because they have a good return for their labor: Ecclesiastes 4:9

Bible Study Groups: *Doing the Bible together*: This would be Bible-centered Small Groups where learning the Word and instructive discipleship is the core. The benefit is being able to grow beyond personal learning by asking questions to learn, hear from others, participate in the text, see God's Word being worked out in the lives of others, interaction to take your knowledge into a deeper level, deepen your love for the Lord and one another, intensify your worship, handle life better, share your insights with others, and be challenged to grow and apply your faith to life. These groups can go through a book of the Bible, explore topical subjects, do inductive study, discuss the sermon, or even read a Christian book, as long as the Bible is the foundation.

Accountability Groups: *Keeping one another in line to His precepts and call*. The main focus of accountability-centered Small Groups is to provide a place to build relationships and be honed by one another. The benefit is being able to interact with others and keep one another on track, to sharpen yourself, and to internalize what you have learned into daily life so God can use you to sharpen others. These groups work best as gender specific--women's or men's groups. Mentoring groups fall in this category of older people who disciple the younger.

Life Groups: *Doing life together.* Share, learn, care, and prayer! The primary function is relational—*how do I deal with life? How do I learn and grow by learning His Word and allowing others to help me encounter Christ and one another?* The benefit is being able to share your life, learn from the experiences and encounters with God others have had, and to feel a part of God's family. This model is excellent for new Christians starting off. It is also excellent for mature Christians desiring to grow further and be further challenged! This type of group works best as a mentoring model for two to five people. Six is too many; when you hit six, start a new group. This type of group can meet as a large group for worship and a short Bible study then partition off into smaller groups of two to four. The consistency of participants is necessary for building community and openness.

I first saw this model over twenty years ago and have since seen it in various forms and acronyms for the name, such as: Living In Faith Experiences and Learning Biblical Truth,

Intercession, Fellowship, Extending LIFE To Others. The key is to be with one another whether that be just prayer, silence (in times of dire stress and loss), or listening. Have an open Bible, a regular, consistent meeting time and place, or just get together sporadically when needed; it is about sharing and caring! When I was on staff with Campus Crusade for Christ in the early 1980's, I helped start the "Lighthouse Movement" based on this model.

Recovery Groups: *Healing and Learning together.* These are semi-therapy groups for people overcoming addictions, life stress, loss, divorce recovery, or learning basic relationship skills. The benefit is being able to deal with life, stress, better being able to overcome extreme hardships such as the death of a loved one, and help in living a more stable life. Premarital and marriage building skills also fall into this category. It is essential that these groups are staffed with educated and trained clinicians or supervised by one!

Ministry Groups: *Doing the service of our Lord together.* These groups are a place to serve and use spiritual gifts. These groups usually have a specific agenda. It could be a ministry in the church or community such as the women's morning break, mothers support, prayer ministry, parenting skills, or direct ministry such as choir, Deacons, Elders, building and grounds, or... The benefit is being able to develop the skills to serve the Lord and apply your faith into the church and community in a more meaningful and effective way. The primary purpose is preparation for the ministry. This is a football huddle, coming together to share, care, and prepare for the ministry by coming to know the Lord and one another more.

Evangelistic Groups: *Sharing the Lord together.* The main function is to invite new Christians and non-Christians. These are Small Groups designed to introduce Christ in a loving and caring way. The benefit is being able to apply the Great Commandment and the Great Commission to the people around you in a personal and powerful way. There are two primary models, the "Alpha Groups" and the "Lighthouses" in chapter 7. (see links in Appendix 7)

> Small Groups are the best way to apply the "one anothers" in Scripture, and there are over 50 of them—look them up in a concordance or see Appendix 4!

There are many other types of Small Groups, too; however, most will fall under one of the above categories. It is paramount and fundamental that all groups must also have the atmosphere of care, be non-judgmental, and be a safe place to reflect on life situations. It is the duty of all participants to give and receive care and learn about the ways of God through the Bible and prayer. Any of these main types can and should combine Accountability and Bible study models with the focus on being interactive and introspective. It is also essential that confidences be kept. What is shared in a Small Group, stays in the Small Group unless you have the permission of the person to share information. (If there is danger, you are obligated to involve a professional counselor and/or the authorities).

If there is little Bible time in a Small Group, the person needs to be in another Bible study group or another primary means for their discipleship. All of these types should incorporate a mentoring model, seeking answers to this question: *How do I deal with life and bring my encounters with God, myself, and others into a more healthy Biblical approach and become a person who learns and grows?* We must allow God's influence and outcome upon us. This means that The Spirit seeks us out, and we grow in Him, allowing His empowerment to affect us so we are affected by Him in our lives for the benefit of our spiritual growth, His Church, and His glory! Each Small Group model—if it is Christian based model—is about pursuing a more meaningful relationship with God while developing key friendships with others in the church. It is learning and growing in community. Remember, we all need to have encouragement, advice, and support from a community of Believers who are growing in Him.

The Key Principles

They devoted themselves to the Apostles teaching and to the breaking of bread and to prayer. Acts 2:42

A Small Group is analogous to a network, an association of relationships joined together in harmony within the bonds of the Fruits of the Spirit, commitment, and a common purpose. The purpose is to know and grow in Christ and make Him known to others in the group, church, community, and world. We are to show our gratitude to Christ by our service to share Him, encourage others with hope and His love through us, help the downcast, and build one another up while proclaiming God's

Kingdom. Within these key precepts, each group will have its own group dynamic (personality) and different skills, call, and opportunities. We can honor their uniqueness and what the Holy Spirit is doing in them, while at the same time, realizing there are key precepts that each group needs to function in its best for our Lord's glory. There is no specific formula or plan for how a church can do Small Groups, as each church and each group is unique. Nonetheless, by understanding these precepts, we can be better able to exhibit wisdom and discernment in knowing what we are to do; thus, the groups can be guided as a shepherd guides his sheep, yet remain uniquely different in Him and used by Him. Thus, the leader and the atmosphere of the group dynamic should have the desire to:

- **Love the Lord!** *Sharing Life's Adventure of knowing Him.* The primary purpose is to encounter Jesus in a personal way. Some will not, and that is OK; we call that evangelism, but the leaders must have this precept down (Mark 12:29-31)!

- **Growing!** *Growing with Jesus* by discovering His precepts and the magnificent person you are in Christ. The group's dynamic should desire to learn and grow in the Lord. Not all will have this all of the time, as we all have our ups and downs in our spiritual pilgrimage, but the overall reason is to know Him (Phil. 3:1-14)!

- **Bible Study!** *Studying the Word.* The Bible is the cradle to God's Word, what He has to say to us. The Bible must be the principle content. The Bible is to provide us with the insights and applications for Christian living. Other topics, such as recovery issues and book studies, may be used as long as the Bible is there--open and used (2 Tim. 3:14-17)!

- **Prayer**! *Prayer* is our means to communicate with God by telling Him our needs and hearing from Him concerning His plan and care. All that we do in a Small Group must point to God as Creator, Savior, and as Lord (Phil. 4:4-7).

- **Relationships!** *Filled with Fellowship.* For celebrating the good times and forming life-long impacting friendships, fellowship is the building of our bonds with one another. We do this by sharing, openly and honestly, and being vulnerable while keeping confidences. People need to know they are in a safe environment so they can share and connect—to care so all can share. This builds trust and community and enables people to be who they are without the need to pretend while they learn who they are in Christ (Col. 2:2-4).

- **Comfort and Counsel!** *Support in the bad times.* We are called to help others through their crises and hurts by listening, and, if appropriate, giving wise council. In the trials of life, we need a place to rest and to heal, and to be encouraged, prayed over, and supported. The result is the healing, learning, and getting back to the game the Lord has called us to play (Rom. 12:1-2; 10).

- **Accountability!** *We are called to hold one another responsible in Christ* within the parameters of care, and to keep confidences (Heb. 10:24-25).

- **Celebration!** *Encouraging and honoring* others because we are in a supportive Christian community that really is, as the name implies, "like Christ" (2 Cor. 2:14-15; 8:23-24).

   When these precepts are at work, all of us--the hurting, the lonely, the curious, the passionate--can come and feel comfortable in sharing, challenged in love, and encouraged to grow in our Lord! In a good Small Group, we can apply God's Word to our lives so we can become what God desires us to be!

   Once the Small Groups are functioning properly, they can be used as outreach and ministry platforms. The people who come to know Christ can now make Christ known!

- **Sharing Out!** *Divide and conquer.* Each person in the group should be encouraged to invite friends and acquaintances (but not forced). The Small Groups need to be open to growth. When they do grow—by inviting new people into them, especially non-Christians—they can split and form two groups, and so forth. The key for success is the training and equipping of the leaders. Leaders should be mentoring their replacements so when the group splits there will be a leader waiting. The leader will teach both by example and by instruction so everyone's potential is sought, challenged, prepared, and reached. Small Group ministry is a team with coaches and assistant coaches who grow to become coaches (Acts 20:20).

- **Outreach!** *Reaching the lost and ministering in His church.* When the Small Groups are growing, they are inviting non-Christians, and can become one of the best avenues to reach people for the Kingdom. Also, the ministry of the church can come from Small Groups, too. Visitation, crisis response, prayer ministry, or virtually any ministry in the church can be operated by Small Group people. Each Small Group can pick a specific ministry and stick to it, or do what is needed when it is needed. This would be in addition to its primary function. The call is to reach people for the Lord and then care for those people and the others in the community and the world (1 Pet. 3:15).

Every day they continued to meet together in the temple courts. They broke bread in their homes and ate together with glad and sincere hearts, praising God and enjoying the favor of all the people. And the Lord added to their number daily those who were being saved. Acts 2:46-47

I believe that these key precepts are needed to create this network to be effective and effectual. Not all these precepts will be in everyone or every group, and this is OK; but, there should--at least--be an endeavor and desire to learn and grow. Sometimes, people just need a place to vent and to express their hurts from the trials they have gone through. Sometimes, people do not know the Lord and are curious as to what this Christianity is all about. Sometimes, people are stagnant in their faith and need to discover how to break their barriers. Sometimes, a person has a passion to learn. Whatever the motivation and reason, a good Small Group will welcome them.

Small Groups are the way to grow your church in faith and use in Christ! Your church is called to build and grow Small Groups!

Now we ask you, brothers and sisters, to acknowledge those who work hard among you, who care for you in the Lord and who admonish you. Hold them in the highest regard in love because of their work. Live in peace with each other. 1 Thessalonians 5:12-13

Chapter 2

Understanding and Developing Christian Accountability

Proverbs 11:14, 15:22, 24:6; 27:17; 2 Corinthians 12:19-13:6; Galatians 6: 1-10; Ephesians 5:21; Colossians 3:9-10; James 5:16

And let us consider how we may spur one another on toward love and good deeds. Let us not give up meeting together, as some are in the habit of doing, but let us encourage one another—and all the more as you see the day approaching. Hebrews 10:24-25

A popular American TV show from the 1960's was *Dobie Gillis*. In this hit show, there was a character, Maynard G. Krebs, played by Bob Denver, better known for later playing Gilligan on *Gilligan's Island*. Maynard was a "beatnik," a precursor to a "hippie" and a pioneer stereotype of the atypical "teenage slacker." He was the person who refused to work, was very lazy, and all of his energies were spent on conniving to get what he wanted without earning it. His catchphrase was "work?!?" when confronted that he needed to work for something in order to receive something. He was very funny and was just listed in the top 100 memorable entertainers of the twentieth century. The TV episodes can still be seen today (my church in near Hollywood and many in the industry attend). Maynard represents a lot of Christian mindsets today—not the fear of work, but, rather "accountability?!?" We fear and hide from it as if it were an assault upon our lifestyle, fears, and plans. We do not want to hear about it, nor be tied to it. Yet, it is essential for us to grow and produce godly character and fruit.

What is *accountability*? It is a check and balance system to protect us from harm from ourselves and others. We do this by being open to what we are thinking and doing so we can receive encouragement and reproof, when needed. Christian accountability is accounting for what we "are up to". It is the realization that we are liable, responsible, and answerable to God for our actions in life (Matt. 12:36; Rom. 2:16; 14:2; 1 Cor. 3:10-15; 4:5; 2 Cor. 5:10), as well as to key Christians in our life (John 13:34 Gal. 6:1-2; Philip. 2:4; Heb. 10:23-24; James 5:16). Thus, we need to hold to our beliefs and keep in line with what we believe so that we are not distracted from God's path for us or discourage others from their path.

Accountability allows us to be answerable to one another, focusing on key relationships such as those with spouses, close friends, colleagues, coworkers, bosses, small group members, and pastors. It is sharing, in confidence, our heartfelt Christian sojourn in an atmosphere of trust. We can give an answer for what we do and understand the need for help in areas where we are weak and struggling, where and how we are growing, what we are learning, and to be encouraged. These precepts help us to stay on track, and get prayer, care, and support when we fail and fall. We can also model guideposts for one another in order to keep going.

> *Accountability enables us to share our lives with one another in a deep, introspective way. This helps us to get to know ourselves and others in a deeper manner.*

Even though most of our relationships in life tend to be casual and superficial, we need deep connections; that is what God has made us for (Eccl. 4:10-12; Rom. 12:5; 14: 13-23; Eph. 5:21; Col. 3:9-10; 1 Peter 3:15). In this, we can have a place to open up, share, and be challenged beyond sports, weather, fashion, or makeup. The goal is our *spiritual formation* which is

Christian maturity, growth, and character derived from God working in us and our working out our faith with one another.

Some Christians have seen accountability groups alone as a place to vent all of their frustrations in life. Yes, we need a place to vent; however, if we are only concerned with venting without feedback, resolution or action, we accomplish nothing. Real growth cannot take place, as the venting will be all-consuming and will leave no time for instruction or feedback. The group will merely become a place to gossip. Accountability is also not a place to find our *inner child, inner warrior,* or *warrior princess.* Accountability is not about complaining about how life has dumped on us or a place to put others down; rather, it is a "compact" (a deeper agreement beyond a contract) and a system on how to become more Christ-like (Psalm 133:1). A good accountability group will have questions, Bible study, prayer, listening, and support at its core.

Accountability is not about confrontation. We may, at times, need to be confronted and to confront another; accountability is more about challenging one another to grow in Christ without the need to rebuke. Accountability helps instill the warning precepts that God has given us; it also has the necessary support, counsel, encouragement, and affirmation we all need. Accountability enables us to be...*in Christ, we who are many form one body, and each member belongs to all the others* (Rom. 12:5). This enables our connectedness to lay aside the island mentality. We do not stand independent of one another. Because such interdependency exists within the Body of Christ, we are responsible to one another to do our part and to help others do theirs.

As it is, there are many parts, but one body. The eye cannot say to the hand, "I don't need you!" And the head cannot say to the feet, "I don't need you!" . . . If one part suffers, every part suffers with it; if one part is honored, every part rejoices with it (1 Cor. 12:20-21, 26).

Why Do We Need Accountability?

We are accountable to God and to one another (2 Chron. 19:6-7; Ezek. 34:2-4; Matt. 12:36-37; 2 Pet. 2:10-11). We are all fallen creatures; as Christians, we are still fallen, but are saved by our faith in Christ Jesus, through the grace of God. We are declared clean before God by our Lord's work; however, we are still sinful. We all have items and thoughts in our lives that diminish our relationship with God and our effectiveness with others. There is still a process on which to embark to become *cleaner* (which I believe we never totally become); this is *sanctification*. As Christians, we are in the process and practice of our faith, growth, learning, and maturity all the days of our lives. At the same time, we are still sinners and susceptible to temptation, spiritual warfare, and our misplaced desires. We have blind spots and need input from others to find them. If you really want to grow in faith and be effective in ministry, you must be held accountable; otherwise, you will fall, backslide, or be ineffective because of imbued pride. Sin will get you; maybe not today, but tomorrow is coming. Accountability is essential for every Christian to help reach his or her full potential; it is a mandate to those in leadership and ministry!

> *Having other people around whom you can trust and get to know more deeply will enable you to know yourself—your strengths, weaknesses, and opportunities—more deeply.*

You will be able to see in the mirror to your inner being and desires and determine if they line up to what God has for you. You will become more aware of issues, relationships, and life as life's purpose and God's call are unfolded before you. Because you see life and God's Word more deeply, your behaviors and response to others will also change for the better (Eccl. 4:8-12; Rom. 15:7; Eph. 4:9-13; 1 Thess. 5:11; Heb. 10:24; James 5:16).

The pages of the Bible are filled with stories of people leaning on others for growth and personal and spiritual development. Deep connections help great leaders overcome their struggles and see what they cannot see on their own. Most prominently in the Old Testament are Moses and Aaron (Exodus), and David and Jonathan (1 Sam. 18-20). In the New Testament are Paul and Barnabas, and Paul with Titus, Silas, and Timothy (Acts 11-14; 2 Cor. 2:12). Our Lord Jesus, while He walked this earth, had His twelve with an extra connection to the inner three, Peter, James, and John.

> *We can surmise that accountability is not for just for those who are weak, needy, or for wimps; it is for the strong*

who want to be stronger and the unconnected who need to be connected.

If you think, "This is still just for the weak", consider that greatness and authenticity cannot come about without humility and connection (James 4:7-12; 1 Pet. 5: 1-11)! "Real men" will be accountable to other real men, and real godly women will be connected to other godly women (Prov. 31). There is no way around this vital call! God gives us the call to be deeply connected to one another because we need it. The leaders in the Bible knew this well, Jesus modeled this for us, and the only hindrance is our willingness to comply. Leaders and pastors who are not accountable will eventually fall, and, until then, be very ineffective! God has called you to be the *iron* that *sharpens* others' *iron,* as their iron will sharpen you (Prov. 27:17)!

Accountability is nothing new. It might seem like something novel, judging by the topics of contemporary sermons and books or looking at some popular movements within the last ten years; however, it was practiced by pious Jewish teachers before Christ. Accountability was insisted on and practiced by Christ, Himself. Observe how Jesus led the Disciples and how He modeled to the Disciples. This was the model for the early church; the Reformers all had men in their lives who held them to account, in whom they trusted, took advice from, bounced ideas off of, and who prayed for them.

Calvin was especially a proponent of accountability and insisted all of His leaders be held in account--"believers (who) seriously testify, by honoring mutual righteousness among themselves, that they honor God." It was the system he established that became the model of the "check and balance" system of modern governments, first established in the U.S. in our Constitution. The Methodist movement, founded by John Wesley, was started as an accountability and prayer group. Every effective minister, leader, and growing Christian I have ever met was in some form of an accountability group, including Billy Graham and my mentor, Francis A. Schaeffer. In fact, I have never met an effective Christian, pastor, or leader who was not in an accountability group. For every bad and ineffective leader I have ever met, none of them believed in or practiced accountability! This should communicate to us loudly our very own need for accountability.

> *The bottom line of why we need accountability is, we will be tempted; unless we have a system to protect ourselves, we will fall to that temptation (Prov. 6:27; 1 Cor. 6:18, 10:14; 1 Tim. 6:9-11; 2 Tim. 2:22)!*

The world is rich in temptations, and we cannot fight against them effectively unless we allow the One who overcame the world to infuse us (John 5:4), and not love the world (1 John 2:15). It comes down to having trusting faith in Christ and allowing His work in others to help keep us connected to Him. His empowerment will be synergized when we are connected with others whom we trust and who can warn us of coming dangers in our pursuits and thinking, encourage us when we are down, and who will hold us accountable. The love of God is often best reflected in the love and care of others. Allow that care to shield you from the wrong pursuits in life.

Many Christians think, *All I have to do is leave Satan alone and he will leave me alone, so I do not need accountability.* The response to that is *No, he will go after you even more!* We will be tempted by Satan and by his influences, enticing and damaging. Satan seeks not to give us what we want, but to steal from us all that which God has given. Thus, if we submit to God, then the devil flees; if we run to Satan and his ways, God is far off from us. We can try with all of our might and effort to have accountability, but unless others are there for us, and unless we are headed toward God, it just will not work! The only thing that can thwart Satan is God. So, be in Him and not in the world (Eph. 6:10; James 4:7-10; Rev. 12:11).

> *James tells us to first turn to God and surrender to His ways. If not, the ways of Satan and the world will gladly take up that role.*

We need others in our lives to point out to us the pitfalls before us, as we may not see them ourselves, blinded by desires and wanderlust. We cannot do this solely by our own efforts and strength; we need others, too. Others will see what we refuse to see or what is blocked by our desires. It is about the insight of others and the power of the Spirit working in us all. It is not the strength of others; rather it is their eyes, words, and assistance, and our allowing God to be our strength. To remove Satan from our lives, we have to fell him—not just ignore him, but run away from him and to God, allowing others to help us in our scurry.

Objections to Accountability

Accountability may seem to go against our self-sufficient, individualistic mindsets and fear of conviction. Many cultures and individuals subscribe to being "my own person," and doing "my own thing." Many people do not like being told what to do or how to do it; however, we need godly people in our lives to do just that—with love and care. Thus, we have to learn to overcome our barriers of conviction so we can grow more in Christ and with one another.

Many Christians see accountability as meaningless because conviction is the role of the Holy Spirit (John 14:17; Acts 1:8; 4:31; 10:45; 2 Cor. 3:18; Eph. 3:16-17; Heb. 13:5-6). Yes, they are correct about the conviction part; they are wrong to say that it does not matter. Why? Galatians tells us to *carry each other's burdens, and in this way you will fulfill the law of Christ* (Gal. 6:2). The meaning refers to moral issues and guarding weakness (Rom. 15:1-3; 1 Cor. 9:21). Take heed; we are also responsible and answerable for our actions in life to God and to other key Christians. Thus, we need to be held to our beliefs and kept in line about what we believe so it does not distract us from God's path for us or discourage others from their own path.

The other typical objection believers give is that we are not under any kind of law, and now we have liberty and Grace, so it does not matter. After I had done a workshop on accountability, a prominent Christian leader a few years back asked me, "*Why is this important? Can't I just live my Christian life as I please? After all, I have liberty in Christ!*" I answered him to the best of my ability, but he just would not get it; shortly thereafter, he fell and fell hard. It turned out he did not like accountability because he had been having a long-term *affair*. He did not want to be convicted! Our liberation is not to protect us from conviction; it is to enjoy our Lord so we can pursue His precepts as we realize our indebtedness to Him.

Liberation simply means Christ has set us free (John 8:32-36; Rom. 6:3-23; Gal. 5:1). Paul was overcome by his liberation in and by Christ (Mark 7:18-19). He stressed that we must behave and be responsible in the correct manner. We many enjoy our freedom, but freedom does not entitle one to do anything one wants, just as living in a "free" county like the U.S.

does not, as we cannot steal or murder or not pay taxes. What about free will? Yes, we have "free will;" Calvin spent most of his writings discussing this fact. He taught that we have *responsibility*, and duty to *faith* and *prayer*--three areas that require free will. We are still to allow His work to continue in us; the Holy Spirit will lift our sin and our will out of the way. If you truly give up your will to God, will you be liberated or would you be obligated as a servant/slave with no real life as you would see it? The fact is that you are free in Christ! The question is *how will you live your life of freedom?*

The liberty of the Christian life is by surrender. It gives us:

1. Freedom from law. (Rom. 3:19; 6:14; -15; Gal. 2:20-21; 3:23-25)
2. Forgiveness, acceptance, and access to His presence. (Rom. 5:1-2)
3. Freedom from having to base our acceptance on our performance. (Rom. 7: 7-11; 10:3)
4. Freedom from sin, and declared cleaned! (John 8:34-36; Rom 3:19; 6: 3- 23; 1 Cor. 15:16; Gal. 3:10-20; 4:21-31)
5. Freedom from our own faulty thinking and superstitions. (1 Cor. 6:12-13; 8:7-13; 1 Tim. 4:1-5)

Because of these five reasons, we respond with obedience—not out of obligation (as a slave does)—but, out of gratitude and love. This new obedience is because of a changed heart and will. We are enabled to respond and continue in our new life by the Holy Spirit. Accountability helps us in our freedom in Christ, because we give up on our self will and focus on His. Like driving a car in a strange unfamiliar area and making Christ a passenger, we, as human beings, spend most of the time arguing, complaining, and debating the destination. Yet, we do not have a clue to where we are going. If we would allow Christ to get into the driver's seat, He would be able to take us where we could never have gone before. In addition, if we sign over the "pink slip" to our Lord Jesus Christ, then He will take us to places that, even in our wildest imaginations, we could never fathom. Then, perhaps the love we are to receive and exhibit will flow ever so much more freely! The bottom line is: accountability is letting Christ drive! Accountability becomes the map to keep us moving on His road to His destination; if we throw away the map, we go in the wrong direction; we will never get to the destination, and perhaps, even crash. It begins when we stop to ask for directions--His Directions!

We are not to allow our liberation and freedom in Grace to cause people to stumble by our actions or inactions. Our faith and actions are monitored closely by God as well as by other people, and we must realize that our actions are more influential than our words. We will either lift people up or bring them down! Hypocrisy is perhaps the most deadly threat to new or weak Christians who fall victim to it, and is a heinous sin against Christ and His children by those who cause it! We, as a body of Christ, must seek to show right actions to one another, to be cautious, and to act with charity, humility, and self-denial within our Christian liberty. We are still called to be responsible in the correct manner. We may enjoy our freedom, but freedom does not entitle us to do anything we want. A true Christian will never destroy another person's faith so he can have his own way! Our freedom must not bring dishonor, division, or disrepute to the church.

The first two objections are from theological standpoints, but what most of us struggle with is emotional—our fears and cultural hesitations. Connecting with others and exposing our feelings may be much easier for most women; but, for men, this is sometimes a seemingly impenetrable barrier. It can be a scary business to share your feelings and be open and introspective, as people may betray us, belittle us, ignore, or step on our hearts. To tell you the truth, yes, that can happen. It has happed to me several times, as close accountability partners have betrayed confidences and spread rumors. However, the benefits have far outweighed the few times I have been wronged.

Women tend to be better at opening up than men, especially generations born before 1965. We were brought up to think that a man is to show no emotion or share feelings—the John Wayne type. This makes a good movie character, but is not good biblical character. We become fearful of sharing our lives with our spouse, coworkers, or even trusted friends. These fears debilitate relational connections and the support we need in life and in ministry as well as hamper trust (Rom. 8:15). Another factor that ties in with this is shame. We feel embarrassed or that we are the only ones going through *this*. We may feel, *"They will reject me when they get to know me. No one will understand. They will think less of me."* The fact is, as growing Christians in

Christ, when we get to know one another, we get to know ourselves as well; love supersedes judgment and care overpowers fear. This leads to forgiveness and openness. If we let our shame and fear rule our emotions and ability to be held accountable, we will not be able to share or receive godly instruction. Sin will rain upon us. When we start to realize that the love and care we send and receive is far better than the isolation we build, it will allow us to grow in maturity and faith because we will be open and honest. As a result, all of our relationships and our ministry will vastly improve.

> *We need to realize we are already accepted by Christ. He no longer condemns us, as, there is no condemnation in Christ Jesus… nothing can separate me from the love of God. Romans 8*

Thus, to be in a Christian accountability group, you are in a group with sinners who all have been wounded, all who fear, all who are saved by grace, and who all are together in exercising the faith. Folks, we are all in the same boat here. We learn of one another's battles which helps us with ours, and our battles help others' with theirs. Insights are gained and shared, and the transformation from fear to maturity commences. Together, we are not to be ashamed of who we are in Christ, living out our faith with passion and conviction. The real shame is a Christian who does not seek help from God and others. Being accountable will promote healing and growth in all aspects of your life!

> *Remember, people will hurt you, because people who hurt are usually hurting themselves; they do not know how to relate. Accountability groups can alleviate the hurt and provide environments that help build relationships.*

What can we do to overcome this obstacle? Be vulnerable, yet discerning. Only allow people whom you already know and trust to be a part of your support group, and advance slowly. Start off with a few of the simple questions and prayer; as you get to know one another, you will build the trust. (I did not do this with the people who betrayed me!) When we feel safe, we are more apt to share; this goes for both men and women. When we feel safe, we better receive essential positive feedback, listen to constructive criticism, and have a longer and deeper prayer time.

The key to effective accountability is to allow our pride to yield to the necessity of being accountable to one another. Our justification in Christ is no escape from bad things happening; the world is still full of sin. It is a starting point to build and develop character, patience, and dependence on God's grace, as Abraham did by faith; we are accountable for our choices. God approves when we are walking in Him! God does not approve when we are walking by ourselves, comfortable in our own petty presumptions, and ignoring His love and truth!

Accountability Can Help Prevent Burnout

Burnout occurs when our spiritual energies are totally exhausted, and we have no will or vitality to make relationships or to complete our tasks. We are worn-out and spent. If we stay in our positions without being refueled, we will throw wrenches into the works, breaking vital components. If you are a leader, your burnout is especially devastating to others because you will be the monkey wrench that sabotages the machine of ministry. We may not desire or be willing to do so, but because of our lack of availability due to the fact that there is nothing left of us, we are of no service; we are, in fact, endangering the vitality and ministry of others.

The stresses of life and the hassles of family will get us down and test our limits; even the best-run family will have this problem from time to time.

So, how can we tell if we're just tired or are experiencing burnout? First, we need to ask ourselves the accountability questions. If we are operating in His precepts, it is probably just exhaustion. However, if we find ourselves being apathetic and detached from our families, we have a problem. We have to be on guard against the most destructive force--pride! Pride and arrogance will produce a superiority complex. We become careless towards others and lose our perspective of what God has called us to do. We can hurt our family, our friends, and, if we are married, we cause intense harm to our spouse. Either the pride, the refusal to set boundaries, the refusal to be accountable, or a combination of the three will cause us to fall into burnout and lead us into sin. We have to be willing to determine if we need an overhaul or just a good night's sleep. A mentor or accountability partner will help us see the warning signs.

24

Accountability Can Help Prevent Stress

You can expect that people at home, church, and work, in addition to your loved ones, friends, pets, and acquaintances will ask you favors for your time, resources, talents, or attention. This is good, and you should do what you can; there will be times when they will deplete you, causing you stress. You cannot be everywhere nor do everything! So, you have to learn how to build a fence that says, *"I love you, but I cannot grant this favor now."* The most important aspect in preventing stress is saying "NO" in a firm, yet kind, way with a simple explanation. That way, you can be better prepared. People deserve a reason; don't just say *"no"*! Be honest, even if you just need time alone. Do not feel guilty; you have to take care of yourself first before you can care for others!

Be aware of stress with family outings and projects, especially during holidays. They are stressful for many people, so take a look at why you are experiencing the same. Why does something cause you stress? Is it your time? Is it fear? Remember, you are not indispensable; if you were, you would need help from a good counselor or pastor! To help prevent many of the stresses of life, learn to plan ahead! For big events, make sure you plan them out ahead of time and delegate! Do not try to do too many things or take on too many projects, especially if they are new to you. If you are a procrastinator (like I am), force yourself to do it early. Once you figure out that life is easier and less stressful when you do things early, you will make it a habit of it. Do not allow people to force things on you just because you have done them before. They need to respect you and your time. Assertiveness is biblical when it is operated within the parameters of biblical character and the fruit of the Spirit!

Accountability helps make us aware of intrusions and stress, but it may take others to see and to tell us to take breaks away from people so we can have more time with family and God. Accountably will help refocus our spiritual awareness and even help our physical energy. Prayer is our big ally to help set boundaries and prevent stress amongst the spiritual and maturity implications! Do not feel guilty! Accountability helps us be aware of anxiety, phobias, and mental disorders that contribute to stress; those can keep us from our relationships and functions with family and church. If accountability is not enough, that is OK. Just make sure you seek help from a good counselor or trained pastor!

Becoming Accountable

Accountability is often associated with a place to be helped with some kind of problem or addiction such as drinking, drugs, smoking, pornography, or some other recovery issue. Yes, addiction can be a principle venue; however, the emphasis should be our spiritual growth which infuses our thinking and behaviors and helps in overcoming addictions. It is not about just overcoming addictions; it is being overcome with Christ as Lord of our lives. We can always wrestle with our temptations through our own efforts, but we might as well be Jacob wrestling with God (Gen. 32). We will succeed as long as God allows and as long as Satan is rendered powerless. Thus, we must flee from him to be in Him (James 4:7-10)!

Effective accountability has the emphasis on building quality and deep relationships that will help us with the following (1 Thess. 5:14 Col. 3:16 Heb. 3:13 Prov. 25:12; 27:17):

As iron sharpens iron, so one man sharpens another. Proverbs 27:17

- Adhering ourselves to God's Word and call!
- Learning to commune with God more deeply so we can respond to His precepts more rapidly and thoroughly.
- Prayer that is not just about our personal needs but also with the needs of others!
- Reigniting our passion for Christ!
- Becoming teachable, and our thinking and behaviors examined!
- Being willing to recognize sin both in our lives and in the lives of others, too!
- Being willing to learn about ourselves!
- Being willing to have healing in our lives!
- Being willing to see the needs of others!
- Being willing to overcome, and to be on guard concerning weaknesses and strengths.
- Being able to trust, share, and commune with another person in depth.
- Being willing to overcome issues that are bad for us.

- Knowing that we need others to keep us on track!
- A willingness to be challenged, convicted, molded, and sharpened so we can change and grow.
- Help to develop better and deeper fellowship and unity with others!
- A platform to be transformed and renewed in Christ!
- Becoming more sensitive and discerning!
- Learning to develop the fruit of the Spirit and exercise it.
- Being willing to confess and hear others in love and confidentiality—without judgment.
- Being encouraged and encouraging others!
- Developing godly, Christ-like character!
- Learning to take risks, be vulnerable, and overcome rejection and betrayal.
- Learning that God has called us to be involved in the lives of others and that we are not to be *lone ranger* Christians!
- Learning that we are to be patient, because accountability is built over time!
- Learning that deep connections do not just happen between services of the church; we have to work at them in community.
- Learning that we are at our best when we are being real and authentic.
- Learning about Christ's redemption and our ability to change.
- Learning we can be used by God to be change agents in the lives of others.
- Learning that relationships require effort and commitment.
- Developing harmony with others so we can communicate, and being transparent without being defensive.
- Developing maturity and spiritual growth!
- Leaning to be humble and wise!
- Allowing the work of the Holy Spirit within us and being used by Him in the lives of others as well!
- The ability to *bust* the noise of our will and desires, as we need a godly perspective we can hear over that noise!
- A reminder that God is in control, even in times of dire stress and confusion!
- Trusting in God and keeping His standards because they are best for us; there is no better way than His Way!
- Understanding that accountability takes place in the crucible (a refractory made of porcelain, used for melting and purifying materials such as gold at high temperatures,

that also refers to the confluence of powerful influences such as intellectual, social, economic, or political) of community with other growing Christians!
- Knowing we need accountability for our support, faith development, and growth!
- Knowing that accountability takes our initiative, commitment, and continuance in it!
- We have no need to hide our sins from those who are entrusted to help us deal with them.

Leading a lawless, indifferent, irreverent life while having a faith that is just fire insurance from Hell may--**may**--save you; however, you will reap dire consequences for this mindset (Deut. 18:15; Matt. 22:13-14; 23;1 Cor. 10:11-13; 2 Cor. 5:11)!

God designed the church as the body of Christ. Thus, we are called to utility and cooperation so we can be there for one another in times of fun as well as stress. We are called to encourage and to equip, as well as hold each other responsible, to the commitment we have made in Christ as Lord.

What to Look For In an Accountability Partner or Group

To get involved in an accountability group, first look for an existing one you can join such as a small group through your church or a neighboring church if your church does not have one. Make sure it is gender specific—men to men and women to women. Most of these groups are found under men's or women's ministries. If none are available or you are not led to one, hook up with another two or three people and start your own. You can find people through a church leader or pastor. In this process, make sure you are in prayer, asking God to lead you in the right direction! The substance of why and what you are doing is more important than the form of how you do it. See our small group channel for ideas, as an accountability group is just a small group with more emphasis on accountability (www.intothyword.org). The key to making this work is for you and the other participants to be open, submissive, listening, and authentic so you can confess your sins in a safe, confidential environment.

What a Good Accountability Program/Person Will Have:

- Look for confidentiality as paramount.

- Look for people whom you already know or have a connection with such as a common interest or season in life.
- Look for people whom you respect, trust, are mature in their faith and character, and from whom you can learn so you can develop closeness and share shortcomings!
- Look for people who maintain a loving and respectful attitude!
- Make sure you use God's Word; it is your standard for faith and practice!
- Make sure no one dominates unless it is a teacher teaching. Have equal airtime so all can be involved. Thus, the number of people to have depends on the length of time you meet. If you meet for an hour, have no more than four people. If you meet for two hours, have no more than seven. If you are in a larger group, have a teaching time, then break down into sub groups for accountability questions and prayer.
- Be willing to be flexible and surrender your time when another person needs extra time and care.
- Participants need to respect the feelings and time of others, and to speak the truth in love.
- Communicate ground rules or a code of conduct, clearly emphasizing confidentiality and equal time.
- Make sure prayer is the focus!
- Seek guidance from others who can shepherd you, who have *been there, done that*—who have "weathered the storms" and are able to share it. Look for people you can shepherd and guide faithfully.
- Seek those who can help you adhere to God's standards rather than to the world's standards.
- Seek faithfulness and constancy!
- Use humor, but not at the expense of others!
- Be committed, and encourage others to be so, too!
- Remember, the primary purpose is to get yourself aligned with God's love, call, and precepts over all else.
- The more mature people must disciple the immature—not the other way around.
- Be aware of your pride, and never allow your maturity and growth to be a source of pride or use it to put others down!
- What you do not want is people who are prideful, who only care about themselves, or who are irritable,

presumptive, "too busy," and neglectful of others! Make sure you are not this way to others!

There is no best way or program to "do" accountability. It can be a "one-on-one" mentorship or a large group that is subdivided into smaller ones; it can meet for one hour or two, once a week or every other week. The important thing is to do it, remain committed, and to follow Christ and not yourself. If you do not "click" with the people in your group or feel you do not have a level of trust, that is OK; this may not be the group or person for you. Look for or start another one.

How can we do this? By seeing others with the eyes of Christ—to see love, compassion, and forgiveness.

Take the *one another* passages to heart (see Appendix 4), and when we do instruct, warn, or even chastise, do it in the parameters of the fruit of the Spirit, without judgment or commendation (as there is no such thing in Christ!). Then, we can be open and honest with one another. God gives us the faith, the strength, and the empowerment to do this, and when we are with others, it is synergized! It is not about our weakness; it is about His strength! When we rely on God and build one another up, we grow in faith and maturity and become more effective to one another. This is reciprocal and will replicate and continue.

So, what is the final obstacle remaining? The commitment to make it continual. Accountability is not just for a time; it is for all times and requires our discipline and dedication to keep at it. If we stop, we soon go back to our fears and complacency. When this happens, sin that before was of no consequence has now grown big and is knocking on your door. Commitment is essential to making anything that is precious work, from a friendship to marriage to being a member of a church. We must be committed and continual. Commitment brings about hope and growth through sacrifice, as we pour ourselves into it while being fueled by our Lord.

The structure is up to you and your group. How do you lead an effective accountability group? The same way you would a small group. Please see the additional resources we have developed for you on our website www.intothyword.org.

Take it slow and easy. Don't try, or even expect, to immediately delve into the deepest, darkest corners of your life. Begin by having your close friends hold you accountable for things like praying regularly and integrity issues. As you see the results and benefits of this, you will also be building up trust, which is necessary for accountability in more personal and private areas. If you need further help in this area, seek a qualified and trusted pastor or Christian counselor. Also, seek someone to whom you can be accountable. Do not just trust yourself; have a small group or mentor ask you these questions on a regular basis!

> *Remember that Christian maturity and character is "Christ-likeness," becoming more like our Lord by living out His precepts. This is not a destination until we are called home to eternity; meanwhile, we who are on this journey must make the most our opportunities. We can learn and grow deeper and closer or we can repel, rebel, and become more worldly. This journey and the road you will take is your choice and in God's providence (James 4:13-17)! So, go and be sharpened, and be a sharpener to others as well! In His Word and in prayer, watch your life grow and be transformed and triumphant!*

Being a disciple of Christ and making disciples requires devotion, nurturing, commitment to the Word, and worship. Most mature Christians would agree on these basics, but other things required include *discipline*, the ability to be studious, and to be accountable. Our basis and starting point is God's character. Peter tells us *"we are to be holy because God is holy."* (1 Peter 1:16), and the way we can respond to this call is by being accountable in our personal lives as believers and as a church. We need to realize that one of our calls is to participate in conflict management so the wickedness of our nature does not get out of hand and so our relationships and opportunities do not fail. God's Word gives us the guidelines and focus for proper confrontation and the management of problems so we can be more effective in His service.

> *Do not allow accountability in your Christian life or in your church to become a forgotten call!*

Accountability Questions can be found at Appendix 2.

But exhort one another daily, while it is called "Today," lest any of you be hardened through the deceitfulness of sin. Hebrews 3:13

Chapter 3

How to Start and Lead Small Groups

For where two or three come together in my name, there am I with them Matthew 18:20

Small Groups are the way to grow your church in Him! Your church is called to make Small Groups!

So what can you do? Start to think small! For God to do something big in your life and in your church, you need to start thinking small—Small Groups! Small Groups are important and essential. They are the primary and best means to learn and grow in our walk with Christ. All Christians who are serious about their faith should be in a Small Group. In the section, "Why we should be in a Small Group," we discussed its importance and impact. Now that we understand that Small Groups are essential for the formation of our Christian faith, we must realize their importance and how they help give us the ability to transfer our learning into real, practical influence to others around us. It is as *iron sharpens iron;* this means we help one another to hone our faith and develop our character. We can listen to all the sermons, read all the best books, buy great CDs, get stuff online, and go to seminars—even seminary; but, unless we challenge one another in the Word and faith, we will only have a shallow understanding of and impact on the Christian life.

Community breeds maturity and growth compared to individualism which tends to breed pride and isolation. Do not get me wrong; we need to be in church under good teaching, we need to do our devotions individually, and be in personal prayer and study. But, to get the most out of our Christian learning so to impact our Christian living, we have to work it out with others who are working it out; and that place is in Small Groups (Phil. 2:12-13).

What Does My Church Need to Do?

Even though there is no set formula, there are a few "tried and true" ways Small Groups can develop that will be more consistent and purpose-filled so they can be more impacting and rewarding for all those involved. Our primary spiritual growth comes from our personal devotional times. Our involvement in Small Groups helps us further our growth and be the "iron that sharpens" one another as each one in the group helps another grow in Him and apply our faith into the world! Make a commitment to develop a Small Group ministry. All the tools you need are in this article, and the rest of the resources can be found in our Small Group channel at www.intothyword.org and in the various links provided in Appendix 7. You can also go to organizations such as Serendipity and Neighborhood Bible Study for good resources. You can see our article on how to start programs. In addition:

- Use our 'Preface' (or any of the Leadership Curriculum from our website on the channel Church Leadership, and of course this is what this eBook is for) to develop your philosophy of Small Group ministry—keep it short and simple.

Have a clear ministry vision of Small Groups and communicate this to the leaders and congregation. This will explain what it is, what it means, its values and purpose, and its benefits. Then develop a structure and plan for it.

- Put in lots of prayer!
- Who will be the facilitators / leaders?
- Who will train the facilitators / leaders?
- What materials will you need?
- How will they be organized?
- When and where will the meeting take place?
- What curriculum will be used?

- What resources will be needed?
- How will the leaders of the church communicate with the Small Group leaders?
- How will accountably be structured?
- How will you deal with problems?
- How will you evaluate it?

Determine how people will be encouraged and equipped, listen to input, and then make the adjustments. Go to the congregation with your passion and plan, and just do it!

Getting Started

Have an 'all church' meeting to promote small groups. Publication in key written and social media, promotion from pulpit, short testimonials during the worship services are key. A testimonial from the pastor and an open invitation is essential. Have tables set up with areas of where people live by dividing up your church by days or areas. Like where people live, use a 'map' and assign small groups to said areas, you can divide by topics and or days of the meeting, like Tuesday meets here, Wednesday meet here…. Assign leaders, if you have them, by a table where to sign up. This depends on your church size, community size and need. You can also have open slots as leaders are 'facilitators' this eases the 'burden' and fear factor to get leaders. Assure your facilitators they will be trained and equipped and you, or a pastor or key leader is there for support and problem solving.

For your meeting, follow above built points. Basically, have a lunch after church, open in prayer, a brief reason why they should be in small groups. A skit or presentation about them, as in act out a 5 min small group. Explain your vision, need, study options and have a Q and A, and then have people go to tables to sign up and then have a short small group by those tables. Have this eBook available for each facilitator. Then they can collect the personal info and determine the start date. Now you have small groups ready to go and equipped to do well!

Marketing Small Groups to a Church That Thinks They Are Scary

The people in your church, whether you have two Small Groups, have never had them, or half of the people are in them, need to be challenged and inspired to be in Small Groups. You have to tell them why they need to be in one, that it is fun and easy, and help alleviate their fears. The pastor must share the passion, personally be in one, and give his testimony.

Further help enable your church membership to get in one by modeling Small Groups through demonstration, skits, testimonies, and literature. Have a table in your church lobby staffed with Small Group leaders to sign people up and answer questions. Once the people are coming, continue the testimonies, share success stories, and honor the people with celebration and encouragement.

The congregation also needs to know how training, resources, pastoral care and counseling will be provided (know the limits of the Small Group; they can provide listening and encouragement but not resolve serious issues or do therapy unless the leader is licensed and trained!) Small Groups can unravel deep hurts and issues that have not been dealt with prior, so people need a place to go to be helped.

Create Clear Leadership Responsibilities!

Have a plan to recruit and develop leaders. Make sure the leaders are growing in their walk, have a plan to deal with problems such as crisis, conflict, and abusive people, have regular meetings for prayer, evaluation, encouragement, and mentoring and apprentice development.

A Model to Equip Leaders

The church is called to find the most capable people possible and protect the flock from potential harm. Never put just anyone in any position; it is better to have empty positions than the wrong people in them! The essential key is for you to find people whose heart is after God's heart (1 Cor. 11:1)! It is always best to find people who have done it before, but this is not necessary, as long as you train effectively. The biggest reason why churches fail at a Small Group ministry is they fail to train the leaders; the result is the occurrence of all kinds of problems (Rom. 12; Phil. 3:10-14, 4:8-9, 13; Col. 1:28-29; 4:7ff)!

As church leaders come together to pray for wisdom on group dynamics and direction:

- Create your own Small Group training booklet; use this eBook, the section on why to be in Small Groups, and how to resolve conflict. You will then have your own manual. Make any needed changes and put your church name on it. (Please keep our copyright info on it, too.)

- Realize that since the dawn of the Church, finding leaders and workers has been a tough task. Our call is to do it even when the results might seem like failure (Matt. 9:37-38).

- Look for a person who is grounded in the Word, has a good temperament, an aptitude and desire to lead, and the willingness to be supervised. If he or she does not like supervision, consider that a red flag warning!

A good facilitator needs to strive for obedience to the principles of God's Word and practice the spiritual disciplines of Bible study, prayer, fellowship, worship, and stewardship. He must have good relationships with spouse, children, friends, church members, neighbors, co-workers. If he does not, find out why; you do not want toxic people in leadership. Sometimes people are shy and that is OK. In addition, these characteristics are very important: an attitude of prayer, a sense of humour, listening skills, a willingness to learn and follow, one who influences people for Christ and is sensitive to others, an organizer, one who is responsible, who possesses an attitude of servant leadership, and one who is willing to explore his spiritual gifts and use them (Matt. 20:26; John 3:30).

- The leader or facilitator will provide the atmosphere of a safe place to ask questions, and be encouraging, loving, caring, and vulnerable.
- The leader or facilitator will come prepared, keep people on the subject, and realize one cannot lead others where one has not been before!
- The leader/facilitator's main purpose is to get the conversation going.
- The leader or facilitator will introduce the subject or text of the Bible and give any background information. (This can be delegated.)
- The leader or facilitator will then engage the group in dialogue to keep the interaction going without dominating the conversations.

- The leader or facilitator will ask questions and help people respond to the passage or subject for a better understanding of the Bible.
- The leader or facilitator will seek to challenge the people to think on a deeper level to discover the precept, learn what it means, how to be a changed person because of it, and then how to apply it to life. He will demonstrate excitement, when people are growing, by giving affirmation.
- The leader or facilitator will inspire by example that we are people in the process of a spiritual journey and growth; no one has arrived yet. He will share life stories, help others discover and apply God's Word, discuss the precepts, encourage—but not force—everyone to participate by asking "what do you think; anyone else?" realizing that there are many times when there can be more than one good answer or perspective to any good question, and be open to the leading of the Spirit.
- The leader or facilitator needs to be willing to drop the subject of the week to address a current stress or crises with a member.
- The leader or facilitator will honestly express the Fruit of the Spirit (Gal. 5:22-23) so everyone can better experience authentic care from one another!
- The leader or facilitator will keep confidences and insist others do the same.
- The leader or facilitator will not be afraid to discuss significant issues about real life.
- The leader or facilitator will laugh and have fun, and plan social outings and get-togethers outside of the Small Group!
- The leader or facilitator keeps his people in prayer during the week!

The key characteristics to look for in a leader are listening, a willingness to facilitate discussion and summarize input, to allow others to contribute, and then practice care, share, be an encourager, clarify issues, give praise, keep people on the subject (unless there is a "teachable moment"—don't allow people to monopolize the group), and handle wrong answers and heretical ideas graciously while pointing out truth (if you do not know the answer do not make up one, research it and get back to them the following week). It is OK to have periods of reflection and silence, as long as you realize that everyone has a right to be heard and to contribute!

We have to be aware that we are led and embowered by Jesus and can do nothing apart from Him (John 15:5). Facilitating takes work and time and not everyone will be able to do it every time. However, a growth in this direction is essential to growing a healthy, interactive group. Remember, any good Small Group that is "Christian" will have the Bible at its core! And, also spend time in prayer for each member and concerns of the church and world.

Types of leaders

Depending how you feel called to structure your Small Groups you can assign leadership functions to one or more people for each group and even rotate leadership in those groups.

Discussion Starter: This person is the primary leader for the Small Group. He can provide the teaching, be in charge of the curriculum, and/or for starting and facilitating the discussion, making sure everyone has a chance to contribute and no one person dominates the group. This role can rotate form week to week, but someone needs to take responsibility of choosing the leaders, curriculum, make sure it flows, and that the right set of course and questioning are being used.

Host: This person provides the logistics, hospitality, a place for the study (preferably in a home), keeps it fairly neat and welcoming, and facilitates the refreshments. Also, he or she keeps a list of the members, takes attendance to make sure absent people are followed up in the week to see how they are doing, provides good driving directions, gets the curriculum out to people a few days ahead of time if needed, and gives an email or call to remind people periodically. This position can also be rotated as long as consistency and the location are known to all.

Prayer: This person is in charge of the prayer to start the group, and facilitate the prayer at the end. This is an important job; each person should have the opportunity to share prayer requests. Keep your pastor, church, community, government and other concerns in prayer, too. It is best to write down each person's request and keep a record of it for seeing answers and growth and to follow up when necessary. Many resources are in our prayer channel under Discipleship.

Other roles can include a **Social Coordinator** as each group should do something fun every other month, like a dinner out, a movie, a trip, a yearly retreat, or? There can be a **Care Coordinator** to follow up on people in times of stress or absence, a **Worship Leader** to provide a few minutes of worship, a **Child Care Coordinator** (I have found that if three or four Small Groups that meet at the same day and time pool their resources to hire a sitter, this provides an excellent way to have cost-effective child care in a central location). The point is that not everything should be done by one person!

> *These people do not need to have theological knowledge or experience; they are the pump primers to get things moving and ask the questions.*

This works best when you use curriculum that already has the teaching and questions in it, such as any of our *Into Thy Word* studies. You can have groups where people take turns to lead; this has also worked well, especially for professionals and moms who are busy. A good leader is a listener and will help everyone get involved in the discussion. Not all will talk; however, there needs to be an atmosphere for dialogue without reproach from others. A good leader will not allow one person, especially him or her, to dominate the discussion unless it is a leader-based Bible study. Even so, community and discussion must be practiced and encouraged.

Basic Small Group Structure

There is no best way to structure your Small Groups, but there are proven precepts that help structure each group for efficiency, learning, and care in the time allowed. Below is a one hour to a one and a half hour model. For a two hour model, add five minutes of time to the teaching, and most of the extra time to discussion and prayer!

- **Warm up:** Serve refreshments, fellowship, perhaps have worship (5+ minutes).

- **Prayer:** Open with prayer, then, have a fun opening question. (The Serendipity Bible is a great resource for this, as well as any discussion starters from Youth Specialties; they work great for adults too.) (5 minutes).

- **The Study:** Curriculum, inductive or...read the passage, then give any relevant teaching that will help stimulate learning and discussion (10 to 20 minutes).

- **Discussion & Questions:** Encourage discussion; make sure everyone has the opportunity to participate, and seek to end with an application (25+ minutes). You an also combine teaching and discussion, buy going verse by verse, tech then discus or reverse this.

- **Close in significant Prayer:** Spend some time asking how everyone's week has been, then spend time fervently praying for one another, the issues from the above categories, and specifics that have come up (15+ minutes)!

Small Groups are usually one and a half hours to two hours; it depends on time constraints and availability of the people. Do not forget to leave room for fellowship. Perhaps you time is 7:00 p.m. to 8:30 p.m., thus you actually start at 7:10 and end promptly at 8:30. This leaves room for people to get to know one another, share life, and fellowship. Make sure you respect people's time.

Then, you need to structure and organize the Small Groups in your church for area coverage, days of the week, and types offered to benefit each member. Also, a leadership structure needs to be in place. For example, for every seven to 10 Small Groups, you need a coach/trainer and a pastor or coordinator in charge of them all. In larger churches, you can group the Small Groups into groups according to where they live under regional coordinators/leaders whose primary responsibility is to train and be a help for the groups in their area. You can have three areas, four to six or more for major metropolitan areas. Make a flow chart, but make sure your chart and structure is flexible and based on prayer, not in feelings and/or personal agendas. It is also best to have regular meetings for group leaders at least every other month for prayer, training, encouragement, and feedback.

Small Group Training

What does the essential training entail? Basically, it is what is in this chapter: "What is a Small Group," "How They Benefit the Church," "The Hurdles," and "Types of Small Groups."

Also focus on The Key Principles and how to resolve conflict (in the Leadership Curriculum and our website on the channel Church Leadership). Typical training can also include:

- Ministry vision, philosophy, and leadership structure.
- A 5 min skit video or demonstration of a small group.
- Various curriculum offerings, training in how to use them, and their Bible content.
- Prayer ideas.
- Group dynamics.
- Interpersonal relationship skills.
- How to care better.
- How to gain new members.
- How to facilitate more effectively.
- How to resolve conflict.
- Prayer.

The Small Groups need to be under the influence of the church and its set parameters, but not over-controlled. Some liberty and freedom needs to exist to allow room to grow and explore other options that the church leadership did not consider. For more insights see: *Training your Leaders and Congregation* (in the Leadership Curriculum and our website on the channel ChurchLeadership.org)

How Do I Recruit Leaders?

So, how do I recruit leaders? One of the best ways to recruit and train Small Group leaders is a "mentor approach." This means to have a primary lead person for each group alongside a secondary lead person. As the group grows, it can be divided into two, and the secondary lead person would become a primary lead person for the new group. Then, a new secondary lead person would be recruited for each group, and so forth.

For additional insights, see our Article on **How to Recruit Volunteers!** (in the Leadership Curriculum and our website on the channel Church Leadership)

Once you recruit the leader, partner them off for a few weeks in another Small Group so they can "get the feel" and give them the training booklet. This provides the model and experiences the leaders will need to have to reproduce the group. Then, meet with them to answer any questions; get their feedback and go over the basics so they have the vision and purpose down. Then, you can supervise, solving problems where and when they occur, reinforce, encourage, and put together more training as you go and grow. Have seminars once or twice a year with all leaders and potential leaders for further training, such as, *how to resolve conflict, and how to interact with the different personality types.* (Serendipity has good resources for this.) You cannot just give them a book, no matter how good it is; personalized instruction and encouragement is essential. If you have a small church and limited resources, partner with other churches and do one together.

- To effectively promote small groups, it is absolutely essential that the main pastor (s) are in one and share their experience from the pulpit and personally endorse and promote the program. Without key leadership support, you are canoeing up a waterfall.

- It is absolutely essential that you be willing and able to weed out people who should not be leading groups. Have them do a personality inventory such as Myers Briggs (links in Appendix 7), and a Spiritual Gifts inventory (in the Spiritual Gifts Curriculum and our website on the channel Church Leadership). Get to know the people who are responsible to care for the flock. You want the flock properly cared for and not fleeced!

- A true leader, one who is in Christ, will have the characteristics of Servant Leadership, an essential trait.

- What should you watch out for? People with wrong or ulterior motives for being in leadership, being over-zealous to lead, have a theological agenda that is not biblical or at variant to what is approved in your church, spiritually immature and/or a lack of willingness to grow, distrust or dislike for authority, or a personality that seems unstable.

- Is experience required for the leader? No, as long as the attitude and willingness to learn and grow are there, he can learn as he goes. Make sure he gets extra support, mentoring, and prayer (John 1:12).

- Having a method of handling conflict resolution is paramount, and will solve most future problems and issues. Firstly, identify the conflict and the responses from each side and listen carefully to them with encouragement and understanding. Secondly, explore a Biblical model of conflict resolution. Thirdly, integrate Biblical knowledge in a step-by-step fashion. And, fourthly, help teach the parties *conflict resolution* to prevent a repeat of such instances in the future. I sometimes bring other staff or other people in if required. I try to eliminate any misunderstandings and have the attitude for a win/win solution.

- Having a conflict-free environment will enhance recruitment greatly, because nobody wants to work in an atmosphere of strife! Alongside this, it is essential to have a Biblical Vision and Mission Statement, so everyone will be on the *same page* of what we do and why we do it.

- Have a public reporting of your progress and growth in the church newsletter!

Instead, speaking the truth in love, we will grow to become in every respect the mature body of him who is the head, that is, Christ. From him the whole body, joined and held together by every supporting ligament, grows and builds itself up in love, as each part does its work. Ephesians 4:15-16

Chapter 4

How to Form New Small Groups

Catching and producing a 20/20 vision for your church!

You know that I have not hesitated to preach anything that would be helpful to you but have taught you publicly and from house to house. Acts 20:20

People are naturally attracted to a program that works and is logical and informative so they can understand it. It is important to create a handout or brochure with your vision and key precepts and how they can get connected in them. This eBook can be that manual; all you need to know is here.

How do I recruit people? Have each group always be open to new people, if possible. Some groups want to be closed; that is OK for them, but for most, having a small group of no more than 8 to 10 participants makes enough room for two more then you can split them up in two. The small group itself is the primary recruitment vehicle and evangelism platform.

The key is to "divide and conquer," so to speak. Each person in the group should be encouraged to invite (but not force) friends and acquaintances. The small groups need to be open to grow; when they grow by inviting new people in to them, especially non-Christians, they can split and form two groups and so forth. The key for success is the training and equipping of the leaders. Leaders should be mentoring their replacements so when the group splits, you will have a leader-in-waiting and so forth. The leader will teach by example and by instruction so everyone's potential is sought, challenged, prepared, and reached. Small group ministry is a team with coaches and assistant coaches who grow to become coaches (Acts 20:20).

The second way to do this is have an open introductory session. This is from Serendipity in the '70's and works incredibly well today. Provide plenty of publicity with 'social networking,' flyers and testimonies in church services and newsletters, then invite all interested people to a "Get To Know Small Groups" event. Do this preferably right after the church service. Make it a short seminar on small groups. Take only one hour of their time and provide refreshments, a light lunch and "smiley" welcoming hosts. In this session, have an opening prayer, a 10 minute message on why they should be in a small group (see section why you should be in a small group), then break them off into tables of 10 according to the area in which they live. Then, have them rehearse a small group right there. Here is an idea: As people gather, give them name tags and on them put a code or color for the area in which they live. Then, ask everyone to go to the corners of the room with their code or color. Next, section them off according to the day of the week that is best for them to meet, and divide those into groups of 10. You can have tables already decorated, such as a Monday table, a Wednesday table and so forth. Why divide into groups of 10? Because. Usually, 1/3 of them will bail out.

Develop a social network group for your church that has intercommunication, that is, each person can share, ask question and the leaders can send messages to anyone and everyone in the group--like a Facebook 'group.' For small groups, each one can have their own too, and you can make them private, although the church main one should be an open group that is monitored. *This is the way most people in their teens through thirties like to stay in touch and it is easy and fun, communication tool.* You can post small groups opening, training sessions, tips, Q&A, and offers for help. You might also use it as a recruitment tool, posting your opening times, places and other relevant messages.

Have leaders there already prepared, if possible. If not, have each group elect a leader and use "user friendly" curriculum. Then, for 25 minutes, have them "do" a small group. Your first session can be about relationship building, a short Bible study, the first four questions in "The Character of Love" study, an inductive study on Romans 12:1-3, or a Bible study on community. (see our small group channel for more ideas.) The people will get to know one another, thus neutralizing any fears. Then, encourage them, and send them off to do a small group for six weeks. Provide curriculum, this article, and your small group handbook or another resource on small groups for them. During the first two weeks, have training for the new leaders. After that, in my experience, most will continue.

You need to have a plan for maintaining the existing small groups so they can be better equipped. If not, the new ones get all of the attention and the older ones can lose their momentum. In addition, you need a plan for how to multiply the groups. You could just tell existing small groups to divide. But, you will disrupt a good group and generate hurt feelings as after a significant amount of community has already been developed, hesitance and resentments will develop. To head this off, make it clear that it is encouraged, but not mandatory, that the groups divide up after reaching a certain number of people. If they know ahead of time that when a group hits the magic number, say 10 or 12, they are to divide, this eases the stress. Just telling them to divide creates undue anxiety and antagonism. If a group wants to stay as they are, then let them do so; never force a program as programs are just a tool of ministry, not the ministry in of itself!

- Have a plan for choosing small group leaders. This process should not just be an arbitrary "get whomever you can get;" these people will be the principle caregivers of your church and must be selected wisely!

- Have a plan for the options and kinds of groups and resources that will be available.

Decide on Bible books, typical studies, recovery, and so forth. Make sure you have the resources for them in your church; do not expect people to hunt for them themselves. Some will do this and like it, but the vast majority need a set of clear options available for them now. Then, provide the training on how to use them.

- It is very important to offer continual seminars and group training. If your church is too small for this, other organizations, perhaps other churches, can do this for you. Perhaps you can go to theirs, but these resources must be offered.

Many new groups do not form in churches because they do not have the leaders. Volunteer recruitment is paramount to effective ministry. Volunteers are best found by personal invitation (see our curriculum How to Recruit Volunteers in the Leadership Curriculum and our website on the channel Church Leadership). It is best to first meet with an interested individual and listen to him, go to a neutral location, or use the church office and get to know each other. Never fill a leadership position with "whomever;" otherwise, you will fail the people in your care! The second thing to do is show him your vision and the plan of action as well as responsibilities and expectations of small group facilitators. Third, if the person has not been involved in a small group, have them sit in on several sessions and observe. Spend the time to train them either individually, or in a group. If your church has more than 250 members, schedule regular training sessions for all small group leaders as well as introductory sessions of training for new small group volunteers and individual follow-up by trained staff members.

Having staff whose lives are centered upon the Lord Jesus Christ is essential in any effective ministry, along with love for the people to whom you are ministering. This creates the atmosphere for attracting good leaders. Concentrate on the training and community building with current staff, along with the recruitment of additional leaders. Focus on building the current leaders to do the bulk of the "contact" work with friends and acquaintances. The "focus is discipleship, and the heartbeat is evangelism," motto applies to recruitment, too. This flows from the primary emphases in leadership, which are building relationships with people and establishing a vision and shared philosophy that instills leadership in the people who are in charge. We need to provide the lead and follow-through with training, love, and resources. I have found it essential, in every position I have held, to develop a leadership team where I am responsible for their training and equipping, because I cannot do the work alone.

Here I am! I stand at the door and knock. If anyone hears my voice and opens the door, I will come in and eat with him, and he with me. Revelation 3:20

Remember: Small groups are the way to grow your church in Christ!

Chapter 5

Small Group Curriculum Model

"Doing Life Together"

My purpose is that they may be encouraged in heart and united in love, so that they may have the full riches of complete understanding, in order that they may know the mystery of God, namely, Christ, in whom are hidden all the treasures of wisdom and knowledge. I tell you this so that no one may deceive you by fine-sounding arguments. Colossians 2:2-4

Small groups are designed to meet the deepest relational and learning needs of the congregation. Small groups can help provide the framework for people to be challenged to worship God with joy, passion, and conviction by learning who they are in Christ so they can develop the trusting faith in Jesus as Savior and LORD. We will be better able to build Christ-centered friendships, and then be equipping others to impact the world—all for our Lord's Glory. Thus, we will be able to pursue our *walk* in Him that builds our *intimacy* with Him, so we are *living* in Him, according to His Word. Our love will be infused with Kingdom principles and not self-desires and aspirations that will only lead to a life of despair. Rather, we will have a life that is triumphant and joyful, fulfilling and exciting, and rewarding in that we become the blessed to be a blessing to those around us.

This particular model is for a relational group, designed to build effective authentic relationships. Learn about them and from God's Word and apply His precepts to daily life. This type of group only needs this article, a Bible and selected verses for the study. A good one-volume commentary or a good study Bible such as the *Reformation Study Bible*, *ESV Study Bible*, and a Bible Dictionary can also be of help. You can also use the *Into Thy Word Bible* study notes too at www.intothyword.org.

You do not need to spend money on books and booklets; most of what is available is not good anyway. All you need is a Bible and a list of the questions in this chapter; see Appendix 1 for a printable and sharable version. This model is best described as a mentoring model and works for all ages. It is great for people and places where resources, such as study guides, are either too costly or unavailable, as all you need is the list of questions and a Bible! In fact, I believe this approach is better than a study guide because it gets our eyes off what one person has to say (the author) and get us more into the Word and serious caring matters in your life from those whom you know care for you! For this to be optimal, this approach must contain basic, introspective questions that search out one's self and become the signposts for our behaviors and our actions and reactions in life. This is combined with what the Bible has to say to us, and we turn to prayer to cement our time in our Lord. Thus, we share, care, learn, and pray. When this approach negates the Word and becomes only a discussion group, it is no longer optimal.

> Without the boundaries and empowerment of God's Word, even with good leadership and discussions, you have just a pooling of personal insights. As good as this may be at times, it will only lead to a pooling of ignorance!

God's Word still must be core here. The Bible Study Small Groups is centered only on the study of the Word with a small amount of time for personal sharing and prayer. This relational group model brings God's Word more into our daily lives so that each person learns from his/her experiences along with the Word, sharing, and prayer!

The Key Principles and Structure

Keep in mind the Key Principles for Small Groups in the section "All About Small Groups!" The qualities and goals for this type of group include, be willing to be a learner of life and the Word. A person who learns, who is usable, and who is not afraid to fail, glorifies the Lord! Be a person who prays and is able to encourage others. You, you will only use a small portion of this curriculum each time you meet, keep track what you did and did not and need to do. Do not feel you have to get through all of the questions in each section (except for the one on prayer), because some groups can spend all the time on one question while another will quickly go through all of them.

1. **Prayer**: Spend five minutes to open the session in prayer; invite Christ into your meeting as if He is there—because He is there (Rev. 3:20)!

2. **Read a short Bible Passage**. Use a concordance and look up the "one another" passages; there are over 50 of them. Or, go through Romans 12 with one or two verses at a time, or John 14 and 15, or, 1 John or James in the same way; use the passages from our Character series. Then ask the Essential *Inductive Questions* (for more inductive questions and curriculums on our Website www.intothyword.org see Inductive Bible Study Basics):

The Essential Inductive Questions

1. What does this passage say?
2. What does this passage mean?
3. What is God telling me?
4. How am I encouraged and strengthened?
5. Is there sin in my life for which confession and repentance is needed?
6. How can I be changed, so I can learn and grow?
7. What is in the way of these precepts affecting me? What is in the way of my listening to God?
8. How does this apply to me? What will I do about it?
9. What can I model and teach?
10. What does God want me to share with someone?

1. **Reflect about the passage**: How is God's Word impacting me, how can He impact me more?

2. **Listen** to one another. Ask how the past week has been. The key is to be open, approachable, venerable, vulnerable, and honest, and keep all things confidential so this is a safe place to be in and to share in! This group is not about looking good; it is about learning to be good! It is about that we all fail at times and need rebooting!

3. **Questions** (Pick a few of these relational questions below and rotate the rest for each week. Remember, Do not feel you have to do all of them or every section (except prayer,) as some groups can spend all the time on one question while another will quickly go through all of them:

   • What has your week been like?

      • Situations that you are dealing with?
      • Good news?
      • Bad news such as setbacks, failures, harm done to me, or what I have done to another?

   • What is God doing in your life now?

      • How is He working?
      • What is preventing Him from working in you?
      • How is your Bible reading and study going?
      • How is Satan trying to work in your life?

   • Accountability questions, choose one or two for each week.

   • Discus the assigned study, passage or devotional reading.

   • What temptations/sins are you dealing with? What are you going to do to resolve them?
   • Is there anything—issues, concerns, ideas you need to share or to confess to?

   • How is your relationship with God? What do you need to do to improve it?

   • How is your relationship with your spouse, friends, co-workers, and church members? What do you need to do to improve it?

- Did you spend adequate time with family?
- How is communication? How can you improve it?
- What is negative in your family? What are you going to do to resolve it?
- What is positive? What are you going to do to honor and reward it?
- How are you maintaining your friends?
- Were you hurt by them this week? How so? What can you learn? How can you bring healing?

- What can you do to improve your relationships, first with immediate family, extended family, friends, coworkers, neighbors and then others around you?

- What is a longing in your heart, an issue or a person?

- What is your dream? If you could do anything, what would you do? What is holding you back? Is it in God's permissive will (not violating His precepts)? What do you need to do to make it so?

4. **Refocus** on God's principles. This is the time to listen to God and His Way. The key to spiritual growth is the desire to grow, the ability and willingness to step up, consistency; eagerness for His Word is essential! If you have not done so yet, open a Bible passage and ask some Inductive questions of yourself; keep it short and focus on "how can this passage change me?" Be willing to learn and obey. Overwhelmed? Then take it by baby steps, a little at a time, learning and putting into practice until you are ready for the next lesson. You can start off using our Character series along with the Scriptures and a question or two from each one.

Questions:

a. Take an issue from the above, use a concordance or your Scripture knowledge, and look up a passage to seek an answer from God's Word. A "Bible Promise Book" works great too; choose one promise for each meeting. You can also use the Scriptures from our Character series (in the Character curriculum).

b. Based on what you have learned this week, what will you do differently now?

      1. What lessons did you learn?
      2. What mistakes will you now avoid?
      3. How can you learn obedience and trust in our Lord?

b. What is something good you have done or learned this week with which you can continue?

c. What Biblical application have you learned? How can this application or insight change you? How are you going to apply it? Benchmark a plan to implement it!

d. What Character is missing from or weak in your life that needs to be implemented or refreshed?

e. What is a bad character you have? What are you going to do to replace it with a good one?

f. How will you exercise the love and care from the Fruit of the Spirit to those around you this coming week?

g. What do you need to do to better equip you this week?

h. What are your eating and exercise habits? Remember, your body is the temple of the Holy Spirit!

i. Are you confident in whom you are in Christ? How will this affect your actions this next week?

j. Do you realize how much Christ loves you? How will this affect you this next week, and affect your relationships?

5. **Resources,** how the group can help, what the resources are that are needed to help in this situation? Remember, listening is essential; do not just jump in and try to fix a problem. Allow a gentle dialog and process to take place so the person is ministered to, not just "fixed."

Questions

a. Do you have any questions?

b. Do you have an issue or habit with which you need help?

c. What resources do you need to help you get over temptations?

d. What resources in time, talent, and treasures do you have that can benefit someone in this group, church, and/or community?

e. How can this group help with support, strength, skills, call, and encouragement for you this week?

f. What suggestions or ways to help with a particular need do you have?

6. **Return**. When will we meet again? How can the groups help one another during the day? How can we improve and grow in prayer, accountability, and accessibility?

   a. Did you connect with someone this last week?

      1. How so?
      2. How did it go?

   b. Do you need a call this week to remind you of something or to encourage you?

   c. What can we do to enrich our meetings?

   d. How do you need encouragement?

   e. This is a good place to assign a passage, a study such as our character series, or a devotional reading for the following week. Agree upon it and keep it short and simple.

   f. When and how can you encourage someone this week?

   g. Who would you like to meet with this coming week?

   h. Is there someone you would like to invite to this group?

   i. Keep the groups under five; when you get six, split it into two and grow it from there. If you break it down into small sub groups for the questions and prayer, you can always meet in a large group for worship and study. Also, keeping the people in the groups consistent and enfolding new people when the groups split helps in the community and sharing.

j.   When will we meet again?

7. **Prayer,** spend time fervently praying for each other and the issues from the above categories along with specifics that have come up!

Remember, you will only use a small portion if this curriculum each time you meet, keep track what you did and did not and need to do.

These groups are to foster support for one another so we can live a life based on Christ and His precepts and values, and so we can demonstrate His character. This is essential for learning how to engage others in community, accountability, taking responsibility, and providing opportunities for witness and service. We learn to be the people of God so we can do the work of God!

This approach can be scary for those who tend not to like to share their feelings and have an aversion to learn from one's mistakes and the input of others. But, this approach is one of the best ways to disciple, to mentor others, and be mentored, as life is about our growth in Him. We will be better able to put character into action and build our spiritual formation. To grow, we need to be vulnerable and allow ourselves to see under the hood of our will and desires, to learn how we deal with life so we can learn from God's Word and the experiences of others, to be more "holistic" (all encompassing, bringing our spiritual life into our daily life) and mature in our approach to self, others, and Christ.

Being in a caring Christian community is essential to spiritual growth as a disciple of Jesus Christ. Small groups are essential for the Christian who desires to grow beyond himself and unto the Lord. This is done in the crucible (a furnace, to process melted metal, a colloquialism of the Puritans meaning a refractory life that is surrendered to God by confluence of life combined with the study of the Word producing patience and spiritual maturity) of community. We all need to be in nurturing

Christian communities that help us to not only grow in maturity and our faith formation, but also help to encourage us so we can integrate faith into our daily lives. If your church is not doing Small Groups, you must ask *why* and *what is in the way*? Perhaps pride?

Small Groups are to be the life-changing framework to allow discipleship and authentic relationships and Christian fullness in your church (Matthew 5: 14-16; John 4:34-38; 6:43-45)!

Do not conform any longer to the pattern of this world, but be transformed by the renewing of your mind. Then you will be able to test and approve what God's will is--his good, pleasing and perfect will. For by the grace given me I say to every one of you: Do not think of yourself more highly than you ought, but rather think of yourself with sober judgment, in accordance with the measure of faith God has given you. Romans 12:2-3

© Note, this chapter originally titled "Life Groups" 1984, revised 2004, *Into Thy Word Ministries* (Gleaned from resources from "Son Life," "Campus Crusade for Christ," "Frontiers Missionary Dr. John Hervey" and the "*Into Thy Word* Inductive Bible Study Method")

Chapter 6

Dealing with Difficult People

For it is commendable if a man bears up under the pain of unjust suffering because he is conscious of God. 1 Peter 2:19

One of the central things that scare people away from coming and leading small groups is difficult people. So we need to keep in mind that not everyone will get along with everyone; personalities will conflict, hot buttons will be pushed, and passions exposed. This is OK; it is about being human. Polite disagreement and tension can enable a group to understand each person's position and learn from them! The leader or facilitator will be aware of this and help motivate people toward the big picture of love and care without putting that person down. There are some precepts from Scripture and tips from folks doing this for decades that I have compiled to assist you.

Let's face it, a lot of people are unreasonable—even Christians. We will run into people who will just not get it or listen, deal, resolve, or handle things God's way. They only want their way or the highway.

Hurting people hurt people! Hurting people will hurt other people! Some people have hard hearts and are unwilling or unable, due to personality defects or chemical imbalances, to see others as God's children. They only see it for themselves. This is very sad; there is not much you can do with them. They are the ones who will be lonely and bitter because that is what they want. We are still called to pray and minister to them, but it is best not to take their attacks personally or allow them to bring your group down and keep others from coming.

At the same time, we have to remember; we all are difficult at times, and we all have sinned and fallen way short of God's standards. That is what the cross is about! That is why it is so important to prepare yourself spiritually and keep your focus on God—not people or situations—so His fruit can work in and through you.

Prayer is the most important act for us in any manner!

Also, remember, your obedience is what is important, not how others respond to you. We are even called to bless these unreasonable people, and we do that by remaining true to His Lordship in our maturity. You cannot be responsible for how others respond and treat you when you are acting in godly character (Romans 12:14-21).

Do not let the situation or the bad people get you down or cause you to become angry or compromise biblical precepts or your character! Never close the Bible or neglect prayer; your spiritual journey and your trust and growth in Him will be your anchor to weather the storms. Do not allow yourself to suffer in your spiritual pilgrimage because of someone else. You are still God's special child (Colossians 3:1-4)! Do not let yourself fall to the world's way, regardless of what the other person does. Give them over to God; He is the one who dispenses justice and revenge, not you (Hebrews 12:6)!

These are the times you need to especially control your tongue and attitude. Focus on the Lord, not the situation. Do not allow yourself to get into a pity party so it is all about you or your hurt pride; it is not; it is all about Him. You may not be able to do anything to resolve the problem in a relationship, but that does not mean you are to give up. Your purpose is to take the focus off yourself and onto Christ as Lord. That way, the bitterness and resentment you got from others will not become a virus that affects you or your small group! Repentance and reconciliation may still come. God is at work, even when we do not see Him. God may use your character to speak to them down the road; no relationship or attempt at reconciliation is ever wasted in His Kingdom!

Preventing Conflict

My people have committed two sins: They have forsaken me, the spring of living water, and have dug their own cisterns, broken cisterns that cannot hold water. Jeremiah 2:13

Most of the conflict we experience in life comes from our selfish desires and our insistence on our own way over and against others. So, we are posed to pounce on each other to get our way, while our Lord looks sadly at our pettiness and calls us to walk above it. But, do we listen? Desiring something is not necessarily wrong, but when we do not trust our Lord for it, then we have a problem. The Bible calls us to come before a Holy God by what Christ has done and resulting from a fountain of *Living Water* which is our Lord. We are to rely on Him and not on our inclinations. When we do the latter, conflict is sure to erupt. When we walk in faith and realize our position before our Lord Jesus Christ, then we will bypass our self-will and yield to His.

Jesus answered her, if you knew the gift of God and who it is that asks you for a drink, you would have asked him and he would have given you living water. John 4:10

We need to understand how evil we are when we fight with each other because of our personal agendas and desires! It is God alone who provides us the *Living Waters*. So, why do we persist in digging our own wells, only to bring up dirt that is useless and worthless? Remember, Jesus IS the Living Water!

We can earn nothing on our own, and centrally, our salvation is a gift from God, so our behaviors with one another must reflect this undeserved, free gift. The *free* does not mean we can engage in war with one another; rather, we are to pursue peace and love.

So, what do we do? How can we restrain our desires to manipulate, control, and to be aggressive, instead of repairing relationships? Simply by realizing whom we are before a Holy God and our undeserving gift! Primary conflict is in us, so we need to control the sin that encroaches us, something Cain failed to do. We must discern between what we desire and what is provided to us. We need to discern between our goals and what the will of the Lord is. We need to discern between what we want and what God wants! Then, the conflicts and diseases of distraction that lead to relationship destruction will cease! Our Lord has already won the ultimate conflict of good vs. evil, of rebellion vs. sovereignty.

How to Deal with Each Kind of Instance...

There are nine types of people, five that can be problematic who give us opportunity for ministry or force us to discipline. These are what many have called the problem people or difficult people. These concepts and terms are originally from my notes form a *Serendipity* training seminar I went to in the late 70's and have modified it over the years from my own experiences and research with some practical and biblical ways of dealing with them.

The Tank. These are the in your face, antagonistic and menacing people that threat and fret for their way. They will try to mow you over with their ideas. They can be accurate but often irrelevant. They tend to be bold and blunt and do not care how you feel and will look for your weakness and then seek to take you down. Do not be daunted, with this type and all types, remember the *Fruit of the Spirit*, at the same time be firm and friendly. Sometimes they just they just want to be heard and do not have the social skills, other times they like to hurt people.

What to do? Ask them to stop, "can you please allow for Suzy to finish, then we would like to hear from you too..." "would you be so kind, to also allow others to speak, so everyone has a fair turn..." ..." let's not interrupt each other and be fair to each ones talk time..." and so to let others discus and other points of view to be presented, then afterwards talk to them. Ask, "How can I help you, what do you need?" If the person continues to be belligerent or stands to shout, remain calm and ask them to sit down. If they continue or explode, ask them to leave the meeting until they can be more civil and that you or the pastor is available to talk. If they persist or come back to the group with the same bad attitude, confront them in a biblical way. If they still are intimidating or belligerent, have another person like a pastor or elder be with you and ask them to leave the group until they are ready to be more sociable and respectful. Do not be afraid to kick people out; if you are fearful, others will leave. You have to remove the wolves for the sheep to function (Gal. 5:19-23).

The Sniper. This is the type of person who likes to make off-the-cuff comments or accuse others of something. Use the same approach as you would to the Tank, and try not to return retorts or use inappropriate humour back to them. Confront them in a general way in public this way, "Does anyone here agree with that?" If they preside, then you can say, "Did you mean to offend or just trying to be funny?" "I want to hear what you have to say, but let's do it in a kinder manner with less offense." Let us remember your code to be respectful to one another; even though the joke was funny, what is funny on TV is not funny in real life. Then, talk to them afterwards—alone--about appropriate and inappropriate humour. Tell them you appreciate them in the group, but we have to be respectful and kind to one another, and give them a copy of the "one another's" (in Appendix 4) and say, "This is the type of group we are about, and we would love for you to be a part of it; if you can follow this code from the Bible, you will not be welcome until you do."

The Land Mine. These are the type of people that just by the way they dress or tone of speech or how they act worry people of what they might say or do, so others in the group try to stride softly when around them. Usually people like that are in a niche social group or seek to startle people, but usually are harmless themselves and try to be frightening so they are not hurt. For them, be friendly and, as the leader, ask them kindly, open questions to get them talking to break the walls down. Kindness will usually move them to respond in kind. If not, please approach them as you would the Tank or Sniper.

The Cry Baby. These people just like to complain, usually because their lives are falling apart, or they worry too much, or they feel helpless in their personal lives. Just like everyone, actively listen to them, so they know they are cared for. Ask them about solutions to their problems, and what resources and helps that can assist them and involve the rest of the group and pastor, too. If they monopolize, ask them, in kindness, to allow others to give input, too. If they are complaining about something you do not agree with, listen, but do not feel you have to agree with them; ask others in the group how they feel. Stay away from political and sport discussions; they go nowhere and just gobble up time and create resentment. Have a policy--no political talk and keep sports to friendly mention.

The Gossip. They are the people who like to be in everyone's business and let everyone else know. On our website, we have a complete curriculum in our leadership, problem-solving page to help you on that. Basically, the Bible, especially Proverbs and James, gives us clear direction on how we are to keep our mouths in God's direction, not our own. What we can do: 'THINK!'

T-THINK Proverbs 16:23, are you? And if you are thinking, is the information TRUE? If the information is not true, then dispose of it. If you are not sure of its validity, then check it out with reliable sources! If a person keeps spreading the slander, then seek out the pastor and or leadership in charge.

H-HELPFUL Proverbs 18:20, is it? Will the information be an encouragement and blessing to the person you are sharing about or sharing to? If not, then do not share it, unless it is necessary to protect someone i.e. telling the church leadership that someone is gossiping and refuses correction.

I-INSPIRING Proverbs 24:26, is it? Will the information convict someone in a Biblical way, and in a positive way? Will the information be uplifting? If so, then give it; if not, then don't do it!

N-NECESSARY Proverbs 10:10, is it? Does the person need the information, or do you need to tell it? If it's the telling, it is of no worth! Don't do it!

K-KIND Proverbs 12:18; 25, is it? Will the information be kind to the person, so in turn you will be kind in giving it?

If someone cannot honestly justify your message to this acronym, then do not say it! Instead, try to say something encouraging, from your heart, and always, if in doubt, PRAY with Psalm 141:3 *"Help me guard my words whenever I say something."* (CEV) Have this "THINK" printed out, and then go to the person afterwards--in private--and remind them of the group code to keep discussions kind and confidential.

Remember what Christianity is all about—grace—and, thus, give them a chance to confess and make things right within the group. If they continue in gossip, use the same tactics as with the Tank.

The Minor Annoyances

There are people who just have bad days, like us all, some have difficult childhoods and personalities that clash, some just are not happy people, overly negative or overly positive. There are people cannot make up their minds and always giving different inconstant answers and do not follow through; others will just sit there and never or rarely talk. Some will only do small talk and never talk about anything deeper. Do not assume that they are shallow; rather, see people as Christ does, broken, hurting people that sometimes lash out and hurt others. They need to see the love of our Lord displayed whether they are new to church or grew up there. Show patience, grace, do not avoid them; rather, keep them in prayer and, if appropriate, guy-to-guy or gal-to-gal or couple-to-couple, invite them out for coffee and get to know them outside of the group.

Keep in mind the people you have are the people God brought you; protect your flock and feed your flock! A pastor I worked with years ago always said, EGR! Extra Grace Required! In God's eyes and many others—you and I, too--are also an EGR's, and God has been gracious to us all indeed. Prayer is a key (Matt. 18:15-17; Eph. 4:15)!

Remember, love covers a multitude of sins; so what shall we do? LOVE!

Love with the love that Christ had for us when we did not deserve it and with the response of the love we should have for each other. Jesus let go of His place with the Father—something of which we cannot conceive. He gave up a precious position for the mission of redeeming us. If we pursued the model that Christ laid before us, how much conflict would we have? Practically none! How could we fight with one another when we are focused on our Lord and the interests of others? How can we carry on conflicts with one another when we take a deep, introspective look into our desires and compare them to the Scriptures?

Our focus must not be in our self-awareness, but on what Christ has done as a template for our behaviors and actions! By being a true example of our Lord, we will neutralize most conflicts. When self-desires are focused on our Lord, intrapersonal conflict will be dissolved; so, there will be no conflict with self-desires. Interpersonal conflict will cease because we will be a community of Believers on the *same page*, especially because we have the interests of others in mind and are willing to follow the biblical precepts to solving conflict. We are left with substantive conflicts between beliefs. When we are a community of Believers with a high view of the Scriptures, we will eliminate most of those conflicts. The conflicts will be between Believers and aberrant, cult groups; the minor theological distinctions can be on an 'agree to disagree' venue. This may sound utopian and unattainable, but this is Christian community in its true, called action!

> *Remember this very important fact; unresolved conflict costs much more than the cost to resolve it.*

In fact, to not manage conflict will enormously cost in your relationships, workplace, and church. It will cost you money, time, lost productivity, shattered relationships, lost children, dissolved marriages, bad decisions—it can literally kill and destroy you and all that you know. It could have been turned around, but nobody wanted to bother with it! Do not let this happen to you, your family, your friends, your coworkers, or your church!

Remember, conflict may be a good plotline for TV or the movies, but not for your life! It is absolutely essential that your small group (s) area haven of rest, not a place for more problems! Be the person who wants to understand the love of God and allow His love to transform you and all of your relationships, this will be contagious!

(More insights on how to resolve conflict are available on our Website www.intothyword.org in the "Church Leadership" Channel and the Sub Channel "Problem Solving.")

Who can discern his errors? Forgive my hidden faults. Keep your servant also from willful sins; may they not rule over

me. Then will I be blameless, innocent of great transgression.
Psalm 19:12-13

You can stop the escalation of hurling verbal weapons that destroy relationships. You have the call and the power to stop the misunderstandings, depression, anger, hurt, frustration, and fears. How? By understanding that Christianity is about yielding—yielding to God—and placing Him and others first. Thus, there is no need to hold the high ground in an argument for attack purposes. Rather, surrender your ground for a common peace. This does not mean that you would be a doormat, letting people walk all over and manipulate you. Remember boundaries and protect the flock when needed; you are a pastoral leader, not a security guard. This does not mean you are being a coward, rather, a person of maturity! This is about placing Christ first as Lord over all. Life is not always about you; it is always about Him—Christ as Lord (John 13:3-4; 1 Cor. 3:16-17)!

Remember the importance of integrity; keep your promises, especially to a spouse and child. Remember the place and purpose of humor; it is to lift others up, never to bring them down. It must not be used to cover feelings or as an instrument used to withdraw from others by using jokes instead of real words of communication.

Handling Judgmental Attitudes

The key is to stay away from seeking or making judgments, such as seeking fault in others and putdowns, focusing on goodness. We all have way too much criticism in our lives from our coworkers, bosses, teachers, parents, siblings, friends, the media, and church members; there is no need to add to it. By curtailing criticism, we will be able to praise, encourage and respect our spouses and the people around us, earning their trust because we have made them safe and secure.

As a leader, set the tone! We will be building our communication through being **respectful**: When we are being responsible we are evolving our relationship, becoming more sincere, learning patience, finding enjoyment, contentment, and building tenderness, faithfulness, understanding, and listening skills: RESPECTFUL! We can build this security by speaking the truth in love, encouragement and listening.

When we do not put a stop to our avoidances and putdowns of others, we will receive the boomerang effect—the criticism and negativity will come back to us. Remember, relationships are communal and continual.

Do I always have to do this? What about if the other person is pushing too much? If you are in an abusive relationship, get out of it, even if it is a marriage. Abuse is physical, mental and spiritual. It is hitting, manipulating and the refusal to stop and get help. Get out and get help, do not let this in your personal life or your small group; kick the abuser out. When the abuse is over and you are confident it will not recur, reconcile. Make sure you have a trusted and trained counselor helping you in the process! Keep in mind the precepts of Boundaries.

> *The bottom line to stopping relationship dysfunction--bad folks hurting your relationships, small groups, or ministry--is to know we do not need to always be defending and attacking others, whether it is a legitimate betrayal or a misunderstanding. Why? Because, our true security is in Christ; when we realize this, we can put up with the dysfunction and negativity of others, and reduce our fears so we can pursue relationships and their healing (Matthew 18:15-17).*

There are more helps and ideas in Chapter 10, *Talking your Way out of Conflict*.

> *Therefore, brothers, we have an obligation—but it is not to the sinful nature, to live according to it. For if you live according to the sinful nature, you will die; but if by the Spirit you put to death the misdeeds of the body, you will live, because those who are led by the Spirit of God are sons of God*. Romans 8:12-14

Chapter 7

Becoming a Lighthouse of Prayer

Using Small Groups for Witness and Evangelism!

"The most effective evangelism tool ever developed!" Billy Graham

Matthew 9:36; Luke 15:7, 11-24; Acts 12:5; James 5:16-17; 1 Peter 3:15

I urge, then, first of all, that requests, prayers, intercession and thanksgiving be made for everyone—for kings and all those in authority, that we may live peaceful and quiet lives in all godliness and holiness. This is good, and pleases God our Savior, who wants all men to be saved and to come to a knowledge of the truth. 1 Timothy 2:1-4

Many years ago I was on staff with Campus Crusade for Christ, and we started this program on how to better reach our neighbors with prayer. Later on, it was infolded into "Mission America," one of our Ministry Partners and the Association that *Into Thy Word* is a part of. It is natural that we have for you a message on "How to Develop a Lighthouse! "

What is a Light House? Throughout recorded history, from the ancient Egyptians to the Mesopotamians and the Greeks, a Lighthouse was, and still is a beacon of light to warn ships at sea of danger and to provide rescue for ships in distress.

What Is A Lighthouse of Prayer? A Lighthouse of Prayer (LHP) is a beacon of light to the wonders of our Lord and Savior, Jesus Christ. He is the Light and you are the lighthouse! This is one of the most non-threatening, totally convenient, simple, yet profound methods of reaching the lost with the Gospel of Jesus Christ. Based on Luke 10, a Lighthouse of Prayer does not talk to their neighbors about God; rather they simply spend as little as five minutes a day in prayer for their neighbors. This, for the past several years, has been the focus of the Billy Graham Evangelistic Association and Mission America, as well as Campus Crusade for Christ.

The Focus is to Prayer , Share, and Care for your Neighbors!

A Lighthouse is a gathering of two or more people, in Jesus' name, uniting together to **pray** for, **care** for, and lovingly **share** Jesus Christ with their neighbors and others in their sphere of influence. Lighthouses of Prayer are places where Believers pray for their neighbors. Houses of Prayer may be in homes, places of business, work sites, college dorms, apartments, prison cells—any place where Believers can gather to pray for unbelievers.

Becoming a Lighthouse is a simple process. We begin by making the commitment to pray for, care for, and share Christ with people in our neighborhoods or sphere of influence. If the notion of sharing your faith of Christ scares you, do not worry because the Lighthouse strategy is a simple way for all of us to share—sometimes without even speaking a word or overtly sharing your faith! Pray with compassion and conviction! But, of course, to really be more influential, we should also open our mouths to what is in our hearts.

The Lighthouse Strategy begins by identifying your neighbors, those you will pray for and eventually share Christ with. The best way to begin is to do a "prayer-walk" your neighborhood. Prayer walking is easy. At least once a week (preferably once a day) go on a walk through your neighborhood, praying for each home as you walk by. Many people pray five blessings upon five homes (a strategy developed by Houses of Prayer). Prayer walking is most successful when you go with another person such as spouse, family, or another Christian in your neighborhood. Prayer for blessings is praying for God's best upon your neighbor's health, family, work, emotions, social life, and spiritual life.

After doing a few prayer walks, begin letting your neighbors know in casual conversation that you are praying for them, and ask them if there is something specific they would like you to pray for. Most people will be glad to give you one or two items. Pray for those items during your prayer walk, share them with your small group or prayer group at church (keep confidences); then, a few days later, ask each person what is happening. Continue prayer walking regularly as you care for and share with your neighbors. Prayer walking in your neighborhood in this fashion begins opening the doors of opportunity. As those doors open, you can show love to your neighbors by offering to do practical things for them that they will appreciate. Begin building bridges. Serve them and meet their needs. Do random acts of kindness—mow a lawn, buy food, baby-sit, look out for a job for a person out of work, send their kid to camp, etc.

The next stage is cultivating common activities like starting block parties, cookouts, sports, and other events. This goes a long way toward building relationships and showing each neighbor you are the kind of Christian that genuinely cares for them. As you express care for your neighbors, you are actually preparing them to receive an important gift that will introduce them to a love far greater.

From this, you can start to develop small groups. Use the Alpha Course (links in Appendix 7), or our Small Group Curriculum Model. Now you have started evangelistic Small Groups!

You can also register as a Lighthouse (link below) to help you in committing to reach the people in your sphere of influence for Christ through this three-fold strategy of **praying** for, **caring** for, and **sharing** with your neighbors. There are further resources that will help you get started in praying for, caring for, and sharing Christ with those around you. This includes video training, tracts, and encouragement.

The Bible urges that prayers, intercession, and thanksgiving be made for everyone. And "everyone" includes our neighbors, whom God wants "to be saved and to come to a knowledge of truth." (1 Timothy 2:1-8) If you are a Believer, if you have neighbors, if you love the Lord and care about those neighbors, and if you have five minutes a day to pray for them, you can start a House of Prayer!

How do we start ?

Start by praying for the "Fives"

- Five neighbors or persons or households who live or work near you, for
- Five minutes a day, for
- Five days a week, for
- Five weeks, with
- Five blessings.

Use the acronym **BLESS** to remind yourself of five important areas to cover when praying for others:

- **Body**—physical needs, health, energy

- **Labor**—work, income, job satisfaction

- **Emotional**—inner life, joy, peace

- **Social**—family relationships, friends

- **Spiritual**—repentance, faith, holiness.

This is a start. At the end of five weeks, you decide whether or not to continue. It does not have to be every day in order to make a powerful difference. As you go, you may start to increase your time.

How Do I Pray for My Neighbors? **Be friendly!** Lighthouse provides a five-week devotional guide designed to help you pray for your friends and neighbors, and a booklet that shows how a House of Prayer can powerfully change your life and your neighborhood. They also have "Door-hangers" and prayer greeting cards—tools to help you connect with those you are praying for, and "Power House," a monthly newsletter full of stories, articles, and ideas about prayer that will help and encourage you.

How can I begin?

Start by saying **yes** to God's call! Then document what you will be doing

Persons I will pray for: write your name below to commit to pray for your neighbors:

_____

_____

_____

_____

Persons I will pray with:

_____

_____

_____

_____

My five-week commitment begins __ and ends the week of__

What I have learned as I have prayed:

_____

_____

_____

Why should I start a Lighthouse?

- The gift you give each person is the Good News about Jesus Christ. There are many ways that you can introduce Jesus to your neighbors. *Lighthouse* is an excellent and easy way to commence!

- Because your neighbors are fragmented, disconnected, isolated, or lost! They need to see God illustrated in the lives of others—of your life!

- If you have no problem openly sharing your faith, use your times of caring to begin probing about the spiritual condition and beliefs of your neighbors. Materials like the "Four Spiritual Laws" from Campus Crusade will help you present the Gospel clearly. See our *Evangelism Channel* for more great resources!

- If you are not sure how to share your faith, then gift giving is the strategy you should use. Giving a copy of the "JESUS" film to neighbors usually results in nearly half of all homes having someone receive Christ. Giving JESUS CDs or "The Passion of the Christ" during holidays can have even greater impact! After you have given your gift, check back with them within a few days and ask them what they thought of the video. You may discover that many of your friends prayed to receive Christ at the end of the CD, but they do not know what to do next. That is your opportunity to lead them in an investigative or evangelistic Bible study for new Believers, or get them involved in your church.

- Ready to Build! Every day new Lighthouses are being established. You can be a part of the growing number of people whom God is using to see their neighbors come to know Christ. They are centers of blessing in which Believers ask the Father for blessings on those who live or work near them.

Can we depend on you to leave His light on from your prayers and example? Let us make our homes "Power House" Lighthouses (Matthew 5: 14-16; John 4:35; 6:44)!

You might want to make a simple slogan, "we are to perceive before we receive." That means we are to engage in prayer before we can accomplish the task. And, when we are in prayer, we come into a metamorphosis that transforms us from the very nature of who we are. Because the first thing that changes for the person praying is the person praying. And, when we are changed, that means our evil, self-desiring nature turns around to become a heart after people other than ourselves. So, we gain the perspective of our Lord and the heart for His people, then the passion to do His will. Then we will receive less opposition from our enemy, the prince of darkness, because He that is in us is greater than he in the world. Prayer is also our shield to protect and defend us from attack and curses. No amount of study and work we can ever do will match the work of our Lord that will flow through us in prayer!

The key is our realization of who Christ is and the power He puts at our disposal for His purpose.

Our Lord told the Disciples firsthand that they would be able to ask anything in His name; then, they lived and experienced it. They did not realize they could do the things they saw their Master do; yet, they did. Do we realize what we can do? If so, do we attempt it or do we shirk at the chance and that His choice is to use and work through us? And, yet, what is our choice? The ministry that our Lord started on this earth continues through us, and through prayer, we receive His direction and power to accomplish it.

Don't you have a saying, 'It's still four months until harvest'? I tell you, open your eyes and look at the fields! They are ripe for harvest. John 4:35

The precepts in this chapter were developed by Richard Krejcir and other staff members of Campus Crusade for Christ ©1982, revised 2004 www.intothyword.org Full permission is granted for its reprint and use.

Chapter 8

Relationships are Essential

I desire to do Your will, O my God; Your law is within my heart. Psalm 40:8

The bottom line for us is that relationships are important and vital and what our life here on earth is all about. Small Groups are all about building relationships! First, establishing and growing a personal relationship with Christ as Savior and Lord; next, getting our relationship with ourselves healthy, and being able to commune with those around us with His Fruit. Jesus called us to be fruitful, not to be nuts! When we realize how important relationships are and taking to heart that Jesus is there loving, equipping and empowering us, we will be able to properly engage in small group ministry and see where we need to go with them.

We can do this with wonder, confidence and without fear, even when we are not sure of the way, because we have been given a plan with which to pilot.

God knows the way. With His Word in hand, and wit the guidance and encouragement from others, we can see the value of relationships and others may be mysterious but they are not foreboding—if we choose to Trust God and use the guide God gives us, the Bible, and not the one we make for ourselves. God wants us to use His plan from His truth.

Why is this important? Because, every connection we experience in life will either prosper or disappear; they will become just loose associations or friendships of real depth and meaning. They either grow us or hurt us, build up or destroy us, and they will either make us content or bitter. The choice is ours as to which "or" will be the direction we go in life. While in this journey of life, we are pursuing and engaging, and the direction we tend to go is usually determined by our reaction to life. The focus and call He has for us is in how we are to treat others and learn from our experiences and setbacks.

Small groups are vital for us to build and hone our relationships. And they are not just about me and how I feel or desire, although these are prime factors; rather, it is more important how I am connecting to and honoring God and His principles to others.

The joy and contentment will be louder and honoring to both us and to others. When the call to reverence Jesus first is heeded, we will start to get what relationships are really about, our connection to Him, and how we bring Him with us to all those around us. It is not about how I am treated; it is about how I treat others! In this, you will see your church prosper and grow in Christ!

When we have the foundation God's Word being taught with truth, confidence, clarity and power in conjunction of small group Bible studies putting into practice the theme of the Fruit of the Spirit, confession, and being willing to learn, we will be able to put into practice the love, friendship, and impact of the Gospel. That way, we take our "or" (which direction I am to go) and proceed in the right direction, which takes us out of the harsh world of confusion and chaos into His Light and Wonder. When we know who we are in Christ, our role in the Kingdom, our purpose, so to speak, all things in our life will be influenced and prosper for His glory. We will have His fullness in us, so His Fruit comes from us to create love and healthy relationships.

When we have love down, we can create character and build good lasting relationships all stemming from our growth and maturity in Christ. Then our "or" goes from despair to prosperity, from associations to friendships of depth. Our friendships, family, church and personal will bloom, our church will become God focused, and our marriages and families will improve. Our "or" goes from hurt to growth, from bitter to happy. This does not happen because of magic words and ideas, but because we are growing and learning and applying our lives to His precepts. This is what Christianity is all about—growth in Him! Your growth sponsors growth in others as His Spirit infuses and empowers us in community.

So much can encumber us. The "or" we choose can easily go in the opposite direction of God's call. We become focused on our past failures and hurts so we do not venture out. We become alone and bitter. All the attention becomes on "me;" only "you" are the focus of your existence. Our churches become havens of gossip and strife; we are left chasing, prideful platforms of the megalomaniacs while Christ is left outside of her doors. As Christians, we are collective and connected in His one Church no matter what creed or denomination; we will be in eternity together, so we might as well get along. Not because of obligation or coercion, but rather to be better ourselves and to please God because of who He is and what He has done for us!

Effective small groups and our resulting growing relationships are communal and essential, compacted, yet simple.

All of life is about relationships, us to God, God to us and us to those around us. Every aspect of life is relational, even the relationship you have with yourself. Relationships are communal because we need one another to have relationships. Relationships are complicated because we make them that way; they are simple because that is how God made them. How we choose to live and build our lives will determine the success and failures of how we relate to others and build lasting, quality relationships.

But God demonstrates his own love for us in this: While we were still sinners, Christ died for us. Romans 5:8

Remember, He loves us; He has our best in mind; His ways are truly best. All of our affairs in life come down to the point of who we are in Him and how we relate who we are to others. How we relate to our next door neighbor, our teacher, boss, coworker, parent, friend, stranger, spouse, and even God all comes from how we learn and grow in life. If we are not learning and growing, we are not building and encouraging. Our success in life is determined from the precepts He gives us, and how we take and apply our lives to God's Word.

The choice is ours to make--simple or complicated, to be hurt or to be happy.

By simply following 1 Corinthians 13 and Galatians 5:22-23, our relationships will vastly improve because of our small groups ministry, we will be acting as God calls us to, and people normally respond in kind to how they are treated. The choice requires our faith in action and our growth in Him. It requires us all to recognize what Christ has done for us so our fears and letdowns do not become our gods and our focus in life. He is to be the focus; He is our God.

We Are Called To a Relationship

Now I rejoice in what was suffered for you, and I fill up in my flesh what is still lacking in regard to Christ's afflictions, for the sake of his body, which is the church. Colossians 1:24

John 15 is the most beautiful description of our relationship to our LORD. He wants us to be with Him! Just as Christ wanted the disciples alongside Him so He could train them, love them, and enjoy their companionship, He wants that of us. He wants love, closeness, and relationship so we can learn and make them contagious. This is our primary call and the will of the LORD. Everything else falls from this prime directive: He loves me! He wants to be with me! Do we want to be with Him? Do we want that close, loving relationship? Do we want to walk as Abraham walked, building altars, placing God first and foremost? Do we want to build our life on the worship of God in response to His promise and His fulfilling of that promise?

'Abide,' or, 'remains' in me are the key words in John 15. We are to abide which simply means we are to trust and depend on Him.

This word, *abide,* is very powerful. It means *God is our dwelling place.* The early Israelites lived in tents in a community under God in the feast of the Tabernacles. It is about collective community and Christ's steadfastness and preeminence, His love and Lordship. He is the One who nourishes us. Because He is the One who gives us our nutrients through His vine, we can dwell in Him, grow in Him, we can flourish in Him, and we can even put up with whatever comes our way in our dealings with one another. As a *branch* that is cut off from the vine is lifeless, if we choose to live our life the way we see fit, we, the Christians, will have no fruitfulness in our lives. In the same way, there can be no fulfillment or abundance when we are away from our union and fellowship with Christ.

Following Christ means that we give up our personal plans and the goals and ambitions we have for our future. Yes, it will be a difficult struggle to leave the plans of our family and friends—our needs—behind, and to humbly follow as a servant to give our LORD the glory with our obedience, doing what our LORD desires over our own ambitions. So, are you willing? Are you eager to do great things for Christ? Consider how important this is for your maturity, character development, and your relationships, which translates to our joy and contentment in life. Following His precepts gives Christ the Glory. When we follow through with what Christ has done for us by letting it flow to others around us, we bring the results of love and obedience. The deeper commitment we bring to our LORD, the deeper impact we have on the glory of His kingdom and people around us.

> *The key to the success of finding and building quality relationships is simple: obedience, willingness to serve God over our needs, and even before we know what the call may be, taking this mindset into life and to others!*

This is also what it takes to empower and build a small group, along with the Fruit and faith Christ empowers us with. God's will for our lives is for us to totally surrender and trust in His power and authority. Abide in Him. He will shape our destiny if we allow Him. He will teach us His ways if we will walk in His ways. Trust yourself to our LORD and receive His call to build yourself and others up!

It always seems easier not to obey, but in the long run it only creates further hardships. Thus, allow your small group to be a platform for relationship building and Bible learning. If you are thinking that this is too much, remember God's supernatural power that He has for us to make it happen. He creates the impossible relationship. Let your relationship to God be as natural as taking a breath so your other relationships become natural. Remember, this takes work and obedience as well as our continual effort and consistence. But, the more we do, the easier it is to do. It becomes even easier when we stop dictating our demands to God and start to commune with Him.

At first, you may clearly see God's will, like in breaking off a bad relationship, or in changing a bad behavior or habit. But, in other areas, it may not be as clear. However, God will guide you by your faith. Small groups and relationships in general are work, but they are worth the work; they are worth the risk even when we fail and get hurt. Do not allow your stubborn nature to rule your will. It is not just what God gives to us that make our relationships grow; it is Christ's redemption and who He is in me. Our call is to respond to Him.

Living our Lives Worthy

If you have any encouragement from being united with Christ, if any comfort from his love, if any fellowship with the Spirit, if any tenderness and compassion, then make my joy complete by being like-minded, having the same love, being one in spirit and purpose. Philippians 2:1-2

Is your joy complete? Have you considered the power and impact the Holy Spirit has on you? Not the grand stances and the show some people put on, then claim it is the Spirit, but the way the Spirit works from the Word of God. There is another spirit the Bible talks about that is important and often overlooked—the spirit of community. As Believers, we are one in Spirit and are to be in one spirit. One in spirit means our connection to one another is to be as in one mind—to be in unity. In the context of Philippians, we are to conduct ourselves as being worthy of citizens of the Kingdom of God as representatives of Christ. One spirit is the result of living in the Spirit and exhibiting the conduct and call of Christ.

"...stand fast in one spirit with one mind striving together for the faith of the gospel" Philippians 1:27

This *one in spirit* is the character of Christ living in us all, making our small groups effective and effectual. The point of the Christian life is not about self-realization, but in knowing Jesus

Christ. It is my recognition of Him in me and not allowing anything to take His place in my thinking, my emotions, and the daily experiences of life. The spiritual and mature Christian will never think his circumstances are merely haphazard, nor will he think of himself as the center of the universe. Rather, Christians are to be Christ-like in what this Philippians passage calls "*attitude*" and in "*form*." Usually, we just skip over such words and miss their depth and meaning. In the Greek, "attitude" in NIV, or "mind" in NKJV, (Philippians 2:5) means a mental state based on feeling, rather than just thinking. It signifies a concern for others; whereas just *thinking* keeps the focus upon us. The opposite of this is "pride," which is what Paul was confronting in these verses.

The characteristics of "nature" or "form" in the Greek mean an "inward character and goodness that is reflected from a primary source." It does not mean a shape, but rather imitating; we are to imitate Christ's character! It comes from Plato's Philosophy of "Imitation," in which he used the illustration of how a fire reflects a shadow on a cave wall, that life and all that we perceive as real is just a shadow on the wall. So, all that we see and experience in life is a shadow of the true reality that is hidden from us. Thus, Paul is drawing upon Plato's themes in pointing us to the ONE true reality, and that is Christ. We only see a mere shadow of Him until we are called home.

This "attitude" and "form" are key words for Paul and what the book of Philippians is all about—not to mention what *life* is all about! This is what helps produce our attitude and relationships. This is why Christ came. Yes, He came to save you from your sins, but then what? Are you to sit in a pew and complain, to throw pity parties when things do not go your way? Are you free to push people away and live a life of discontent? Are you to hate those around you or be a loner? NO! NO! The Holy Spirit is determined that we realize Jesus Christ in every aspect of our life. This means all aspects! There is to be no part of our lives cut off or off limits to His work. If not, He will bring us back to the same scenario repeatedly until we learn the lessons He has for us, and until we get it right.

Whether we do menial activities, like raking leaves, or tackle big projects for the church, the mature Christian will see everything as Christ does, even in those times when it seems He has "dumped" on him. Thus, our daily activities, as well as those bad circumstances such as stress, setbacks, failures, and such, are a means of growth and learning and becoming more like Him. We are to see all that there is in life as a journey to further secure the knowledge of Jesus Christ in our lives, even to the point of being recklessly abandoned to Him.

After that, he poured water into a basin and began to wash his disciples' feet, drying them with the towel that was wrapped around him. John 13:5

When He walked this earth in human form, Christ Himself realized His relationship to the Father even in his normal, day-to-day activities. Jesus knew that He was God, but as a man He "took a towel," the most low and menial task of His day. It would compare today to our washing a toilet. Can you imagine Bill Gates going down to the warehouse and washing the dockworkers feet? Or going to their homes and cleaning their toilets? Yet, Christ did, and He is God, Creator and Sustainer of all things! So, if the Creator of the universe was able to be humble and be guided by the seemingly small voice in a loud and large world, why cannot we?

Self-realization is thinking that we are *all* that leads to the believing. We are the centers of the universe. It is in thinking that if we are good, we will go to heaven, or that we are good persons, and we work hard, so we do not need Christ in our lives. It is saying that "if He is there, we will keep Him on a "short leash." This is total anti-Biblical thinking. When we have this mindset, no growth will accrue. There will be no maturity, no seizing the maturity of the Christian life, and no partaking in the real meaning of life. Instead, the focus in life is on the trivialities, desires, pleasures, eating, the drinking, or chasing the latest fun and not the example of our Lord as He demonstrated in the washing of the disciples' feet. We forsake each other for ourselves or use others as a means to gain status or whatever it is we desire. The Holy Spirit is there all along, trying to guide us in, calling us to relationships like an airport attendant with two flashlights guiding in a jumbo jet. The pilot must keep a careful eye on the person guiding him as well as the controls of the aircraft or else the multi-million dollar plane and the hundreds on board will be in dire jeopardy. We, too, must keep watch on the Spirit and His guiding, a teaching that is clearly seen in these verses.

We must watch. We must give up the controls so He can steer our lives His Way, our ministry His Way, our relationships His Way, lest we crash, resulting in consequences to all those around us.

Jesus Christ is our Pilot, not a copilot, navigator, or traffic controller. How does one do this? By keeping our eyes on Christ as LORD. It may come small, like a small man with an even smaller flashlight as compared to the monstrous 747 jet. However, the 747 cannot park in the dark, nor can the passengers go on their way without the guidance from two very small flashlights. We have to take the initiative of realizing Jesus Christ in every phase of our daily life. If we do not, a counterfeit will invade in the place of Jesus.

...that at the name of Jesus every knee should bow, in heaven and on earth and under the earth, and every tongue confess that Jesus Christ is Lord, to the glory of God the Father. Philippians 2:10-11

One of the chief goals of being in a small group and leading one is our spiritual formation, to grow in Christ, in the faith and in maturity of faith and relationships. The aim of the mature, spiritual Christian, who desires to live the true Christian faith, is to have this Christ-like theme imprinted upon his heart and mind. This theme will permeate every activity and aspect of his life from preaching a sermon to washing a toilet, from buying groceries to leading a person to the Lord, *that I may know Him* (Philippians 3:10).

Do you know Him where you are today? If not, you are failing Him. This may seem harsh and un-Christ-like from what is popular in the pulpit today, but very biblically true. Let us not be confused in our culture, our desires, our needs and wants, or our ideas of what we think the Christian life is to be like, and let us surrender ourselves to what the Word is really calling us, to maturity and growth in Him!

We are not on this earth to just appreciate ourselves, but to know Jesus and to make Him known. In our evangelical Christian subculture, the trends in thinking are too often placed solely on the idea that *something needs to be fixed and I must be the one to do it.* Yes, something must be fixed, work must be done, and we must do it. Nevertheless, we do it, not just for the aspect of work, but because of whom we are and what we have been called to do—mature and grow. What usually needs to be fixed is me! We need to allow Him to fix us. When everyday Christians are pursuing the heart of Christ by following His character in *attitude* and *form*, then we will see our relationships change; then our churches will change and then society will change. It all begins with you saying, *I will abide in His work!*

That I may know Him. Do you know Him where you are today? If so, what can you do to implement the Christ-like character? If not, what is in the way? Takes this to heart; what we experience in life, what we go through, what we suffer through, what we give up is all just a mere shadow compared to the eternity to come. What we seem to lose is of no comparison to what we gain in Him! Christianity and suffering are the ultimate in *delayed gratification*!

Do you know Him so that your direction and source of inspiration comes only from Christ? Most of us will look to our creeds and confessions for that answer and for good reason. But, I want to challenge you to go deeper in your faith and personal responsibility. That is, *how do I take my faith so seriously that it becomes more personal, so it becomes more real, so all my thoughts, ideas, directions, goals, and inspirations are in the direction of serving our Lord?* To take your faith to a deeper level, so it is about *abide*, so it is yours and personal and not just because this is what your family is and does, not just because you are part of a good church and school or work, that your faith is solely because of what Christ has done for you and nothing else is solely the work of the Holy Spirit! But, we have a responsibility to respond, to grow and build on what we are given! It takes trust, faith, and surrender of your will, surrender of your dreams, and surrender of your ideas to the LORDSHIP of Christ. You must acknowledge that He is Lord over you by His love for you, and that His ways are better than yours. Christ is our King, so let us live our lives in response to what He did for us!

Building your Life on the Rock of the Word

Therefore everyone who hears these words of mine and puts them into practice is like a wise man who built his house on the rock. Matthew 7:24

In this Matthew passage, Jesus is closing the Sermon on the Mount with the importance of application (Matthew 5-7). This passage implies the contrast, found in Proverbs, of building a house of wisdom versus the folly that can destroy it. It is His final message, in this discourse, on precepts for living our life to the *maximum* and building the Kingdom of God. He states that it is useless to call ourselves Christians unless we practice what He has taught us, which we are to believe and also teach. Some have stated this is a utopian approach to Christianity, one that none of us could ever achieve, while others have taken this stance further saying, "*Why should we even bother with something we cannot possibly do?*" But their error is that we can do it, or Jesus would not have called us to His precepts in the first place. We may fail; I know I have, but we are still to follow through to bringing His utopia to the best of our abilities. If not, we are only building on sinking and shaky sand. We will just fall.

To achieve more intimacy with and function for our Lord, we must be willing to take a look at ourselves to see where we are and on what foundation our lives are built. This passage tells us where we lay the foundation for our life. What is it that moves, stimulates, and inspires us? Will we be able to weather the storms of life, or will we be washed away? Is our life built on shifting sand, the ways of the world that distract us and lead us away from Him? Does everything we consider to be valuable and important just wash away from the stresses, chaos, misdirected deeds, and bad decisions of life—from SIN? Or, do we build on His foundation and from the precepts of His Word, where we remain steadfast and secure?

> *When we build on the Rock, we are securing a firm foundation with our obedience and trust in what Christ has done, as we put it in all aspects of our life.*

So, our motivation is based on who we are in Him. This is not done by our proclamations and speeches, it is manifested by taking the knowledge of our Lord and His work, and the relationship we have with Him so it becomes the transforming force to motivate us in all other relationships. If all we have is knowledge, we have nothing. We are just fat sheep, perfect for the kill by our enemy, as a fat sheep cannot function well. If all we do are *works* in His name, without the knowledge of who Christ is, we have nothing. We have to have the knowledge and put it to work, make it alive and relevant. Thus, doing the

Christian life and building healthy relationships requires us to be totally bought by our Lord, transformed by His grace, and living out His precepts to the best of our ability, always striving and always willing!

To weather the storms of life and to please and glorify God, we must be real, authentic Christians, whose lives are transformed and built on His foundation as we will be tested in life in preparation for eternity. Being only a "fair-weathered" Christian who has never struggled or who has never taken seriously his/her faith may soon find out that he/she had neither faith nor a relationship with Christ as Lord! So, do you?

But the one who received the seed that fell on good soil is the man who hears the word and understands it. He produces a crop, yielding a hundred, sixty or thirty times what was sown. Matthew 13:23

In Matthew 13:23 we have two key words that strike at the foundation of our compliancy, *hears* and *understands.* These two words tend to convict and challenge us where we may not like to go, as most of us do not like to listen, and especially, we do not like to carry it out. But, this journey takes us on the road of His will, His love, and His best for us and those around us. Jesus calls us to wake up and do something with our faith, not to just sit in a pew and complain, or lay on a couch as life drifts by. A call is pronounced. An action must take place to secure His precepts to be an impact; we cannot just hear we have to obey. Obedience is not in words, but in deeds that demonstrate our words through practice and action. This is not about our salvation; it is about our worth and our impact. Our salvation by faith alone may secure us, but for what impact if we do nothing with it? When we read and/or hear the Word of God, as His elect, we will have the desire and heed the call to put it into action.

Yes, there will be times we do not feel like it. Life is tough; it is full of setbacks and hurts that seem to cripple us.

So, we go on permanent disability, when Christ is there with His healing power. We ignore Him and go on hurting; and, in turn, we hurt others. Yes, we will hurt we will need times to recover, but we must make the determination to recover and not stay disabled from abiding in Him. Obedience will override our feelings so we do remain steadfast and secure. We can praise our Lord because He heals! He takes those of us, who are broken hearted, and holds us, cares for us, and encourages us to keep going.

In Jesus' time, the teachers of the Law would debate which was more important: hearing, or doing the Law. Some taught that all you need to do is hear and memorize it, while others held to the fact that you had to do it, too. The argument that won out at the time was that if you did not hear it, you could not do it, so, hearing was more important. Jesus uses their words against them as He did in the other themes of His sermon. As we know, from actually reading the Bible and not just debating it, both are necessary. You must first know it, and also apply it, which applies to the Christian, his/her faith, and the Word of God.

We have to have more in our spiritual arsenal than just belief. We have to have more to grow in Him and make our relationships work.

Our faith cannot just be academic or an idea, or even just a hope; it has to be real. Judas was an example of a person who knew about Christ. He had the knowledge and firsthand experience that we do not have; yet, he did not put it into practice. To him, Jesus was just an idea and a hope for his agenda and purpose. Judas was not willing and thus not able to *abide.* When his storm came, he failed, and betrayed his Lord, so his house fell away. His foundation was sand, made of the gains of false expectations, misplaced hopes, false ideas, and a skewed determination. He knew the will of God, but he did not obey the will of God.

In verse 24 of Matthew 7, we see the word *house*. It is not about a building or a residence or even a home. Yet, it is something we build. *House* is the life you build, who you are, and how you respond. The *foundation* is the thinking, teaching, doctrine, or philosophy to which you subscribe. Life is what we make of it; He gives us the materials and it is up to us to build. We can build just about anywhere we desire to, but will it be the right foundation and place? Jesus' point was to encourage people to get out and do what He was teaching by contrasting the difference between those who are just listeners and not doers. We have to ask ourselves, *what about me?* We are the *builders;*

we all will build our lives and form our relationships! The question is whether we will be wise or foolish builders. Will our house stand up to the storms of life?

The *storms* are the tests and situations we will be faced with, from minor hurts to major illness, loss of friends to loss of loved ones, the mistakes we make, financial setbacks, what others do to us and our sin, our decisions, or other principalities and people acting against us. God knows the storms are coming, but what do we do? The hearers of Jesus' parable knew you have to prepare even though Palestine is basically a desert and storms are very infrequent. However, when they do occur, they come up fast, without warning, and are very tremendous (Matthew 8:24-25). A few years ago in the city where I live, a housing development was built on a flood plain. The flood plain was clearly marked in the city records and the builder and investor knew about it, and it was even near a canyon and a river. But, since there had been no flood in the past two decades, they surmised it was worth the risk and to go ahead and build and hope there would be no flooding. Well, soon after people moved into those homes, the floods came, the damage and distress came, followed by the lawsuits, the media, and the blame shifting. Where we build is important; it does matter now, in life, and resonates in the eternity to come.

The passage goes on to say whoever *does not do them* is a fool. This does not mean just being stupid; it is a reference to judgment. We all will be ultimately judged, and when we hear and do not obey, there will be trouble. Our deeds will be as worthless as a love song with no love in it (Ezekiel 33:30-33). When we hear something from God, we have the responsibility to put it into action by changing our mindset so it affects our behavior, strengthens our faith, and motivates others as well. Our character development will be the quintessential test of how we weathered the storms and built our foundation, because our character becomes the essential building material that helps us weather through those storms and even takes the storm's substance to build even more perseverance! Unlike weather storms, the tempests we go through actually give us the stronger and better materials to add on and remodel our house to be better and stronger. I say this out of love, not out of condemnation; it comes down to two choices, to *abide* or to *ignore*, sand or rock, *well done, good and faithful servant...*

(Matthew 25:21) or *you wicked and lazy servant...* (Matthew 25:26). Which will it be for you?

When anyone hears the message about the kingdom and does not understand it, the evil one comes and snatches away what was sown in his heart. Matthew 13:19

In any population, people will build wherever they can, looking to the moment and not to the long term. The city where I live in Southern California has building codes that help protect people from their shortsightedness. In many poor desert regions today, such as in India, there are few to no codes, so people build shanty homes in flood plains out of desperation or ignorance, thinking they are safe for a time, until the rains come down and their homes are washed away. Where the builder in my city did it out of greed, they tend to do it out of their perceived necessity. And, I have seen this firsthand too many times, as so many lives are literally washed away. We, too, wash away our own lives when we build in the wrong place and with the wrong materials. When we ignore the Word of the Lord, we will be left out in the storm. The storms come for the foolish, those who do as they please, without forethought or faith, and they will face the destruction of their houses. All they are and have can be totally annihilated because the ways of the world and its lies become their refuge, shanty homes built on shifting, foundationless sand in a flood plain. You can hide from God and do as you please for a time; sooner or later, the rains will come to you! We must allow God to be our shelter from the storm. Like an unscrupulous building contractor who builds on a flood plain, or with shoddy craftsmanship, the storm will reveal the real quality of character. Real goodness will outlive and outlast any worldly imitation.

Not as the Scribes

Woe to you, teachers of the law and Pharisees, you hypocrites! You shut the kingdom of heaven in men's faces. You yourselves do not enter, nor will you let those enter who are trying to. Matthew 23:23

In verse 29 of Matthew 7, *not as the Scribes*, was a putdown to those who like to just sit and talk and do nothing with it. The Jewish leaders placed their trust and faith in their knowledge, but did nothing with it. Their comfort was who they thought they were because of their position and acceptance in society, and the show they made with their works. They held onto the faith of their forefathers, but rarely, if ever, confessed that faith themselves. Rabbis would often go as far as to quote one another as their proof text to back up their arguments. Yet, they did nothing with it. The Pharisees had the Scribes transcribe their new laws called the *Mishnah*, a collection of commentaries and insights to the first five books of God's Word, going back to the time of Nehemiah in 400 B.C. and continuing through the third century. The *Mishnah* is revered; it is almost worshiped, yet not put into practice. The Jews still have this today as one of their main commentaries. The other main book the Jews use, besides the *Torah*, is the *Talmud*, which is made up of commentaries on the *Mishnah*. This is so sad when used only as commentary and insights without action to accommodate it.

We Christians do the same with our skewed focuses, traditions, and misdirected motivations, while our opportunities and relationships go distorted and slip away by the sands. For example, in the *Talmud*, there are 156 pages devoted just to the observing of the Sabbath as it applied to life! So, the Jews placed traditions and rules on top of traditions and rules, covering the original rules of God with their own roadblocks of reasoning and self-proclaimed devotion. Many Christians do this, too. We place so much emphasis on tradition that we forget what it is and who it is we are to worship and do church for. Then, we do this in our own life as our past experiences can become our personal traditions that form a pattern we keep repeating. If it is a bad pattern, the repetitions will be bad; if the pattern is good and based on God's precepts, then we do well.

We can see how serious the Pharisees were about keeping the Law. They wrote down all of the laws, such as the Ten Commandments, then applied layers and layers of duties and commentaries over them, so the original meaning eventually became lost. Thus, when a rabbi wanted to speak on a topic or give a sermon, they went to the *Talmud* as their first and sometimes only prime source and not into the actual Word of God. Their authority was tradition and building more tradition. Jesus went straight to the Word with Himself/God as the authority, which astounded people. As a Christian, we are always to teach what the Word of God plainly says, adding none of our false presumptions or traditions. We have no teacher in Jewish history who taught with the authority that Jesus did. Authority was reserved for the Law itself, whereas Jesus came to fulfill the Law. Let us abide in His authority.

God's Word is the material for our growth and life. He hands it to us, and we create even more building blocks by our trust and obedience. But, the key is we have to engage in and continue the practice.

I cannot tell you how many times people have come to me and said their relationships were not working or they did not have any close relationships. After listening to them, I quickly discovered that they do little to nothing to work or pursue them, for which I also was once guilty. For some reason, they expected God to provide a wife or husband, give them a best friend, or provide the ideal coworkers and so forth, dropped from heaven, right in front of them. Now, I would not say that God does not work this way, because I have seen things dropped right in front of me and others, but the usual way this works is we have to pursue them.

Our small group relationships are a responsibility, not only in connection, but in our committed persistence. Building healthy relationships does not always come naturally; in fact, I rarely seen them come naturally. It takes effort, determination, persistence, and the pursuit of God.

Then he said to them all: "If anyone would come after me, he must deny himself and take up his cross daily and follow me. For whoever wants to save his life will lose it, but whoever loses his life for me will save it. What good is it for a man to gain the whole world, and yet lose or forfeit his very self? Luke 9:23-25

Chapter 9

Understand the Importance of Prayer!

One day Jesus was praying in a certain place. When he finished, one of his disciples said to him, "Lord, teach us to pray, just as John taught his disciples."He said to them, "When you pray, say: 'Father, hallowed be your name, your kingdom come. Give us each day our daily bread. Forgive us our sins, for we also forgive everyone who sins against us. And lead us not into temptation.'" Luke 11:1-4

Real Prayer is Saturation Prayer

This passage in Luke is not a prayer, but rather a model for us to follow on how to pray. The closer we follow this passage, the closer we come to our Lord. The closer we come to attaining the fullness of our spiritual potential, the better we pray. As members of the body of Christ, it is our responsibility to be always teaching one another how to pray. The best teacher is the one who models it in his or her life. We are to model this in all activities and pursuits in the church. We are to be specific, simple, and follow the above aspects, so that our prayers are relevant and not too general or crude. We must be honest and open with our Lord and our will needs to be opened because of what He has done for us, who He is, what we wish to do, and who we are to Him. Then, we can share our burdens and intimacy.

Prayer is pivotal and essential. Prayer must be a vital component of any healthy small group and leader!

Prayer is meant to line us up in His will and with His empowerment. Being faithful in prayer is the essential mechanism for reaching others with the faith. Nothing of value can accrue in you or through you without prayer. These Scriptures, Matthew 9:35-38, John 14:12-14, and Colossians 4:2-6 testify to us that we need to be praying for workers, for ourselves, for opportunities, and for those who do not know Him.

Prayer is our key to God's door. It is our foundation to the exercising of and growth in the faith, and essential in our witnessing.

It is the work of Christ through the work of the Spirit that saves. Prayer lines us up to His will and grows us in maturity and understanding. It is the power behind, in the mist of, and in front of the faith. To be effective in your growth in Christ, you have to be a person who prays—and prays regularly. To witness, you must be praying for that person's soul and conversion. Pray as specifically as you can, and as often as you can. It may take a few minutes; it may take many years. Whatever the cost and time, *prayer is the foundation to any work of evangelism.* Without effective prayer, you cannot be effective in your evangelism—**period!**

Do not even try to lead or minister without prayer. Sharing your faith without praying for the person is like training a pig to fly; all you will do is waste your time and annoy the pig. All you will accomplish in trying to do evangelism without prayer is distance yourself from God, waste your time, and annoy the person. Why? Because you are trying to do the work of God without God.

If you think that you do not know how to pray, you need to ask yourself, *do I know how to talk and listen?* If you know how to talk to another person, you know how to pray! Prayer is basically our communication with the Great, Sovereign God of the Universe who wants the best for us and who wants to hear from us. The great wonder is not so much in how we pray, but that God is willing to listen to us. The great, wonderful *fallout* from our redemption is our ability to pray real and effective prayers that God actually hears and to which He responds. God will actually speak to us through His Word; the Holy Spirit teaches and convicts us through the Word. The fact is, our prayer time with God is basically our conversing with Him, through which we express our gratitude for whom He is, what He did for us, and how we can discover our purpose in life. Thus, through our prayers, we can be taught, we can grow, and we can be convicted so we can apply His precepts to our lives and affect those around us, too. This then transfers to the people God lays upon our heart to reach, connecting with Him before we connect with them.

> *Prayer is not just talking to God. It is also meant to further link us to Him and develop our relationship with Him so we can build our faith, character, maturity, and then our witness. Remember, we have access to God; we have permission to come to Him! Wow. What a privilege we have!*

Practical Strategies for Praying for Small Groups

Devote yourselves to prayer, being watchful and thankful. And pray for us, too, that God may open a door for our message, so that we may proclaim the mystery of Christ, for which I am in chains. Colossians 4:2-3

1. Know this important point: No amount of corporate prayer will make up for a lack of personal prayer. That is, you can and should pray as a group, but because you pray as a group does not mean you can cut back on your personal prayer time. Your personal prayer time is the key to your growth in Christ.

2. There is no better use of your personal and ministry time than prayer!

3. There is a phrase that says, "Familiarity breeds contempt." Sometimes, the people we are close to have hurt us even betrayed us; perhaps we just do not trust them, perhaps we fear their response, or perhaps we just do not care. We have to have a heart for someone before we can be an effective

witness. Continue in your character development and spiritual growth, be consistent, and allow your changed life to show without words—even when others do not respond well to you. Start to pray for them. Then, when you have a heart for them, start to be in prayer, pray more, and then use your words to witness. Do not witness to people you have contempt for, as your attitude will show. All that will accomplish is to give the Lord a bad reputation and make it harder for the next person. Wait until you have the right attitude. As the stewards of the airliner says, "first put the mask on yourself before you put it on someone else."

When I went through the training at the *Billy Graham School of Evangelism* and "Crusade Training," the point was made that of the over 90% of the people who come to a Crusade, 95+% of those who go onto the field and pray to accept Jesus, have been regularly prayed for by others for a significant period of time.

Be a Small Group of Prayer!

What is the essential thing to do before each activity, meeting, or event at your church or potential church? Pray. Prayer is the platform on which plans begin, end, and rest. There should never be anything that goes on at a church that does not have prayer at the central core. Remember confidentiality. Prayer requests are not ammunition for gossip. If your church is not a church of prayer, your church is not healthy; it is not in God's will, nor is it focused on Christ. Your church is a mere club for the prideful.

Pray that I may proclaim it clearly, as I should. Be wise in the way you act toward outsiders; make the most of every opportunity. Let your conversation be always full of Grace, seasoned with salt, so that you may know how to answer everyone. Colossians 4:4-6

Pray Specifically!

1. It is essential that all those on staff and leadership of your church be people   of continual prayer. If they are not persons of prayer, then they should not be   in leadership.

2. Begin each meeting in prayer, and spend at least one-fifth to

one-third or more of that meeting in prayer. You say you do not have the time? Well, most meetings are taken up by poor preparation, not following the curriculum, and trivial discussions that go in circles. Have the notes given out a day or even a week before and require all to read it before the meeting. Then, by putting the focus on prayer, meetings actually go faster because people will be of one mind and direction. (Well, mostly.)

3. Spend significant time in prayer between meetings about the needs that have been shared. Prayer will move the focus away from our perceived agenda to His agenda. We then can surrender selfish ambitions to do what is best for His church.

4. Have a specific people pray before each meeting, just pray. Before the event, for safety, get specific requests from the members. You should do this for all ministries and activities of the church.

5. Once a month or so, have prayer walks through your neighborhood.

6. Have assigned people to pray for each pastor, and missionary of the church on a constant basis. Do this for both individual prayer warriors and, collectively, for a prayer group.

7. Have a trained team of people to pray for people after each Bible study and church service. That way, a sufficient number of people are partaking so no one is being rushed.

8. Fasting is for today! It is not a tool to force God to comply, but for us to comply with His will.

9. Once a year try to have 24-hour prayer vigils on a regular basis, where two or more people are at the church, potentially praying all the time. (Do this in short sessions so they do not "burn out.")

10. Have "Concerts of Prayer," on occasion. That is, have a prayer service with directed prayer and silent prayer. Pray for revival, for individuals, for government, etc.

And pray in the Spirit on all occasions with all kinds of prayers and requests. With this in mind, be alert and always keep on praying for all the saints. Ephesians 6:18

The best prayers tend to be targeted to specifics. God is a God of details. He knows them, and He wants you to know them too. Prayer is not only for when it is convenient or for short periods of time when we can remember; prayer is to be continual and persistent, the occupation of our soul. It may start small, but as you pray, it will grow. Your persistence is key.

1. Hold your relationships up in prayer. For individuals, find out (without gossip) needs and concerns, and then pray. While in prayer, look for opportunities to share.

2. Identify any demonic influences. These are called "strongholds" and include cults, temples, sin-based businesses such as adult bookstores and sleazy bars, and pray against them. Satanic strongholds are the devil's campgrounds to war against the work of God. Satan cannot take any ground that Christ will not allow.

3. Find out the problems and needs of your city such as adult bookstores, false religions, poverty, fatherless families, jobs, and corruption. Pray as you walk, pray at home, and pray at your church.

4. You can take the strongholds down simply by focused prayer. Pray as you walk by them, pray at home, and pray at your church. Strongholds are not fringed, charismatic things; they are biblical precepts.

5. Make sure you have confessed your sins and repented before you dare do this. Repentance is essential; after you repent, you can resist the devil. So, be prepared for a backlash to your efforts. Keep up the prayer with your eyes and resolve focused upon Him.

6. Do not condemn or judge others for their lifestyle or decisions. Such actions by us are not biblical or fruitful.

7. Remember, the more you pray the more you will be used. Your fulltime job will to be to pray for these with whom you are to share the love of our Lord.

8. It has been my experience in church planning and evangelism that it takes at least one month of continual prayer before your witness is effective.

You will find more prayer resources on our website at www.intothyword.org located on our *Prayer Channel.*

Pray: *Let us, oh Lord, be willing to learn about you, to grow by your example of obedience and be willing to go through times of waiting, confusion, discouragement, and even suffering and see your precious opportunities of personal growth, faith building, and strengthening.*

Prayer is the essential key to any ministry; if you are not praying, you are not communing with God or being used by God very much!

"Father, I want those you have given me to be with me where I am, and to see my glory, the glory you have given me because you loved me before the creation of the world." John 17:24

Some passages to consider: Proverbs 30:8; Matthew 6:5-15,19-34; 7:7-12 18:21-23; 26: 36-44; Luke 11:1-4; 18:1-8; John 17; 2 Corinthians 12:7-8; James 2:13; 1 John 1:9

Chapter 10

Talking your Way out of Conflict

Here is a roadmap to help yourself and your church, through the Biblical process of solving problems in small groups or in any situation!

As a pastor, I get involved with every kind of conflict imaginable, from business disputes, personality clashes, monetary discord, land rights, probate, parent teacher issues, and of course, the most common, marital. I learned over the years, not so much from my degrees in psychology but, rather, my pastoral experience, how to talk my way out of problems. Being a person who hates conflict, I seek the easiest, most efficient way to put it down. I had to, for the sake of my survival and sanity, figure a way to focus others on the relationship more than the issue. This worked great for many years in pastoral ministry until I came across domestic violence. These other issues were not life threatening, until I came up against people in enraged situations trying to literally kill one another.

For some strange reason, a person who hates conflict (me) had the opportunity to be a Chaplain for a Southern California Police Department for a couple years. My role was to ride along with and minister to the officers, and accompany them to the most dangerous police call there is—not bank robbery or dragnets—domestic violence. I spent a significant amount of time in training for this, and as a *man of the cloth,* so to speak, enraged couples were more agreeable to settle down without violence in my presence than for a uniformed officer. I had to learn fast—as my life and the officer's life depended on it—how to dissolve violent situations. These precepts, along with my pastoral training and experience, can be of help to you, too.

This is not the avoiding of problems, although I have been known to do that, but by carefully listening and coming to a solution to appease the person, the situation can be calmed down so the facts can be evaluated. Then, the concentration can be on the building of the relationship. Otherwise, the problem will continue and the relationships will suffer. The most important thing I had to learn is to not take problems at face value so that they overwhelmed me. I had to see the big picture—that God was still sovereign, and this, like any storm, would eventually pass and be forgotten.

Most problems seem complex; intertwined with so many people and so much hurt and communication ills, it seems overwhelming and hopeless. But, that is not the case; most problems have just a few simple components to them that can be isolated and dealt with. Even when I arrived on the scene with a man chasing his girlfriend with a knife, I was able to resolve the issue without shots being fired. Of course, you should never engage in a violent situation without significant training and someone at your side who is armed. But, you can resolve many issues in your life and the lives of others with a few simple hints. If you are not the one to do this, it is OK; most pastors should not; they should refer people with problems that they cannot handle to a good counselor or lawyer. And, with violence or potential violence, always, always call the police; do not take a chance. It is better to have a false arrest than a dead body!

Here is a roadmap to help yourself, your church, or a moderator through the Biblical process of understanding and solving problems. This can be easily applied to church conflicts, business disputes, and martial (Proverbs 3:4-6; 18:13; Matthew 15:18-19; 18: 15-20; Luke 19:1-9; 1 John 14:15; Romans 8:28-29; 1 Corinthians 6:1-8; 10:31-11:1; Ephesians 4:22-32; 5:1; Philippians 4:2-9; James 4:1-3):

Essential Points to Remember:

1. **You are Christ's loved one** (2 Corinthians 12:9-10): Do not take the problem as a personal attack, even if it is. You may be a part of the conflict, or a third party trying to resolve it. You are Christ's child; He is your identity and defense! When you understand that, you can better see your role as a relationship builder—even when the other person is seeking to tear you down. This first point has saved me a lot of stress and disappointment!

2. **Conflict is an Opportunity** (1 Corinthians 6:1-8): It is an opportunity to learn and give God honor. It is not necessarily bad or the end of a relationship. Know for certain that God can use conflict, whether it is sin, bad choices, a wrong turn, or a misunderstanding, and transform it into good if you let Him. God will be glorified, and you will grow in character, maturity, trust, love, obedience, and in faith.

3. **Listening** (Proverbs 28:13; James 1:19-25; 1 John 1:8-9): The first job is listening, without opening your mouth. Effective listening and getting each party to listen is essential! Until each one listens, nothing productive will happen. People need to be heard; the one who listens earns the right to be heard and resolve the issue. Make sure they know you are listening by giving eye contact, leaning forward, and being relaxed. Restate to clarify what you heard with as few words as possible, saying, *this is what I heard...* Be open and say, "I'm confused; let me try to restate what I think you said." Or, "You have said so much; let me see if I have heard it all."

4. **Understand Forgiveness** (Psalm 103:12; Isaiah 43:25; 1 Corinthians 13:5; Colossians 3:12-14): Most Christians have a pale sense of the wonder that we have been forgiven, and often fail to show that forgiveness to others when wronged. Forgiveness is absolutely crucial for any relationship to continue, and critical to resolve any conflict! Remember how much you have been forgiven; do not fail to show it to others! Remember, God does not treat us the way we tend to treat others.

5. **Communication** (Luke 15:11-24): Seeking understanding is more important than resolving the issue.

Most issues do not need to be resolved if all parties can understand one another's situation. Get them to talk and listen, and you are on the road to recovery! *Why is the person hurt? Why do they feel that way? What do they want? What can be done?* How to do this:

a. Pray for and wisdom and discernment! Keep praying, gather all of the facts, and get second opinions and godly council without revealing confidences.
b. Be positive, have a win-win attitude, smile, and look the person in the eyes. Affirm each person; make them feel comfortable. Let them know you care and want to hear them. Treat each person with utmost respect and kindness even if you feel they do not deserve it. Remember that they are God's children, too! Operate in the Fruits of the Spirit, not the works of the flesh!
c. Do not be afraid to give the moderation over to someone else if you cannot handle it. I have done this many times over the years, due to time, family, being out of my field of expertise, and personality clashes.
d. When you confront, ask yourself, "*How would I want to be confronted?*"
e. Be humble and introspective so you can understand how you, or (if you are the moderator) the participants have each contributed to the conflict (Proverbs 19:11).
f. Never compare your life and situations with that of others; God deals with everyone equally, yet differently. Think before you speak (Ephesians 4:29)!
g. Write stuff down!
h. Validate each person as important.
i. Use humor only when it is appropriate to diffuse a tense situation and never as an attack!
j. Identify each person's involved interests, concerns, desires, needs, limitations, and fears.
k. Allow all the parties equal time to tell their side without interruption; get feedback from the others.
l. Do not be self-focused; focus on the issue, facts, feelings, and how this affects Christ's Kingdom and Fullness.
m. If you are a part of the conflict, speak for yourself—not for the other person! As a moderator, make a ground rule that each person can only speak for themselves and not reword or restate the other's view. The finger pointing is stopped and listening can begin.

n. Attack the issue, not the people; allow no condemnations, commands, threats, condescending attitudes, name-calling, or disrespect!

o. Commit to understanding one another and each person's side, and to refrain from interrupting.

p. Phrase the problem as questions and not attacks! Phrases such as, *you feel* (state the feeling) or *because* (state the content) are appropriate.

q. Do not blame! Have each party state how the issue affects them, how they feel. For example, if a spouse is always gone and the other is angry about that, state, "When you are gone I feel... (Lonely)," rather than "you are never home." This diffuses most arguments and refocuses the blame to how they feel. When each one is aware of the other's feelings, especially in martial conflict, problem solving can begin.

r. Ask, "*How is the problem dishonoring God? How is it hurting each person involved and how is it damaging the relationship?*"

s. Be open and willing to listen to all solutions no matter how ridiculous. Again, people need to be heard! This invites the willingness to cooperate and listen.

t. If people refuse to talk to one another, have them write their complaint on one page with a general description, their side, what they think the other person did, and their solution. Then go over it, summarize it, and present it to both parties. Do not allow them to respond until it is fully read.

u. When sin is involved, it must be confessed and dealt with. The person's attitude that promoted the sin needs to be addressed and confronted.

v. Make sure you are listening and each person knows you are listening. If you are the moderator, you can restate each person's response. If it is a marriage situation with only the couple, restate your position in a positive way by saying, *this is what I heard...* When you summarize, do not add new ideas or your agenda!

w. Keep to one issue at a time; do not allow other past conflicts to interrupt. When multi problems are raised, it becomes too frustrating and overwhelming to solve. Solve one, or at least come to an understanding, before going to the next one.

x. Say, *What can we do to solve this problem together? What are the steps do you see that can resolve this issue?* If that does not work, place the issue on what the purpose of the Christian life is about, to worship and glorify Christ. *How can we develop a solution that glorifies our Lord?*

y. If the parties or you cannot calm down, take a break; if that does not work, reschedule for another time.

z. Start to work together by seeing each person on the same team and not opposing adversaries; we are all God's children, and in the same church family.

6. **Commit to a Positive Solution or Understanding** (James 4:1-12; Matthew 15:18-19): A lot of conflicts, especially marital, will continue as each person is constantly "pushing buttons;" they are on a merry-go-round without being merry. You have to make a decision that the pushing will stop, regardless of the hurt, for the sake of the relationship. Ask, "What can we both do differently to solve this problem so it does not continue?" Then resolution can begin. All parties must agree that the cycles of conflict must stop. Unless there is an agreement and a follow through, no resolution will take place. Sometimes, problems cannot be resolved, and that is OK if understanding can be sought. If the person refuses to stop escalating the problem, they are too steeped in pride, and this problem has to be referred to church elders and/or civil authorities. In the case of domestic violence, this is where I would "cuff and stuff them" into the patrol car. In the church, this is where they are asked to leave the fellowship until they get right with God.

Break down the issue in steps and then come to a solution that all can agree upon.

a. Gather all of the information you can. Write down the facts, feelings, possible outcomes if unresolved, and possible outcomes if resolved. Look for root issues; most problems are symptoms of deeper issues.

b. Write down the description(s) of the problem.

c. Write down what positive result each person would like to see.

d. Evaluate and summarize each person's statement so it describes the situation fairly.

e. When you are dealing with substantive issues such as money, property, or human rights, you need to involve an attorney or professional in that field to help resolve the issue. If it is a theological issue, adhere to what is plainly taught in God's Word and your church confessions. But, even here, the goal is to be cooperative, not competitive (Matthew 7:12; 22:39; 1 Corinthians 13:5; Philippians 2:3-4).

f. Brainstorm possible solutions by thinking through ideas without critiquing them. Evaluate; do not argue! This is the *what are the possibilities* stage; you do not need to jump to a conclusion. Take your time.

g. Look at all the ideas, and then ask, "How might we come to a mutual solution?" "How can we create a new and better future?" Remember, all are on the same team!

h. If this is a conflict involving you, if there is no moderator, and if things are not going smooth, be humble; find a trusted, mutual friend, counselor, or pastor to moderate! Do not allow your pride to push others away and destroy relationships!

i. Now evaluate the ideas one by one. What are the advantages and disadvantages of the ideas? Which ones are acceptable to all parties? Which one glorifies our Lord the most? Remember to keep it positive; not everyone will be happy.

j. Create a schedule to implement the best possible solution.

k. Remember, when people are uncooperative, only God can change them and they need to have the willingness to allow Him to do so (Romans 12:18; 2 Timothy 2:24-26).

l. If you failed to come to an understanding, take this to heart—as long as you are obedient to Him, you did not fail; you succeeded immeasurably! Some situations cannot be resolved, simply because of pride.

m. Once an agreement is reached, commit to the fact that this incident does not need to be brought up again, especially in marriage. *I will not complain about it, I will not dwell on it, I will not gossip about it; I will not use it against the other person. I will forgive and forget and move ahead in building our relationship!* If not, it will just start all over again!

Dealing with difficult people (1 Peter 2:19)

A lot of people are unreasonable—even Christians. We will run into people who will just not get it, listen, deal, resolve or handle things God's way. They only want their way. Some people have hard hearts and are unwilling or unable, due to personality defects or chemical imbalances, to see others as God's children too. They only see it for themselves. This is very sad and there is not much you can do with them. They are the ones who will be lonely and bitter because that is what they want. We are still called to pray and minister to them, but it is best not to take their attacks personally.

We have to remember; we all are difficult at times and we all have sinned and fallen way short of God standards. That is what the cross is about (Isaiah 59:1–2; Matthew 5:48; Rom. 3:23; 6:23)! That is why it is so important to prepare yourself spiritually and keep your focus on God—not people or situations—so His fruit can work in you.

Prayer is the most important act for us in any manner. Also, remember, your obedience is what is important, not how others respond to you.

We are even called to bless these unreasonable people, and we do that by remaining true to His Lordship in our maturity (Luke 6:27-31; Ephesians 4:29). You cannot be responsible for how others respond and treat you when you are acting in godly character (Romans 12:14-21). Do not let the situation or the bad people get you down, or cause you to compromise Biblical precepts or your character! Never close the Bible or prayer; your spiritual journey and your trust and growth in Him will be your anchor to weather the storms. Do not allow yourself to suffer in your spiritual pilgrimage because of someone else. You are still God's special child (Colossians 3:1-4)! Do not let yourself fall to the world's way, regardless of what the other person does (1 Peter 2:12 -19; 3:15b-16). Give them over to God; He is the one who dispenses justice and revenge, not you (Hebrews 12:6)!

These are the times you need to especially control your tongue and attitude. Focus on the Lord, not the situation. Do not allow yourself to get into a pity party so it is all about you; it is not; it is all about Him. You may not be able to do anything to resolve the relationship, but that does not mean you are to give up—especially in marriage. Your purpose is to take the focus off yourself and onto Christ as Lord. That way, bitterness and resentment you got from others will not become a virus that affects you! Repentance and reconciliation may still come. Remember His timing; I have seen miracles of reconciliation long after I had given up hope. God is still at work, even when we do not see Him. God may use your character to speak to them down the road; no relationship or attempt at reconciliation is ever wasted in His Kingdom (Psalm 10; 37; 1 Samuel 24:1-22)!

Preventing Conflict

Most of the conflict we experience in life comes from our selfish desires, our insistence on our own way, over and against others. So, we are poised to pounce on each other to get our way, while our Lord looks sadly at our pettiness and calls us to walk above it. But, do we listen? Desiring something is not necessarily wrong, but when we do not trust our Lord for it, then we have a problem. The Bible calls us to come before a Holy God by what Christ has done and resulting from a fountain of "Living Water" which is our Lord. We are to rely on Him and not on our inclinations. When we do the latter, conflict is sure to erupt. When we walk in faith and realize our position before our Lord Jesus Christ, then we will bypass our self-will and yield to His.

"My people have committed two sins: They have forsaken me, the spring of living water, and have dug their own cisterns, broken cisterns that cannot hold water." Jeremiah 2:13

We need to realize how evil we are when we fight with each other because of our personal agendas and desires! It is God alone who provides us the "Living Waters." So, why do we persist in digging our own wells, only to bring up dirt that is useless and worthless?

"Jesus answered her, if you knew the gift of God and who it is that asks you for a drink, you would have asked him and he would have given you living water." (John 4:10)

We can earn nothing on our own, and centrally, our salvation is a gift from God, so our behaviors with one another must reflect this undeserved, free gift. The *free* does not mean we can engage in war with one another, rather, to pursue peace and love.

So, what do we do? How can we restrain our desires to manipulate, control, and to be aggressive, instead of repairing relationships? Simply by realizing whom we are before a Holy God and our undeserving gift! Primary conflict is in us, so we need to control the sin that encroaches us, something Cain failed to do. We must discern between what we desire and what is provided to us. We need to discern between our goals and what the will of the Lord is. We need to discern between what we want and what God wants! Then, the conflicts and diseases of distraction that lead to relationship destruction will cease! Our Lord has already won the ultimate conflict of good vs. evil, of rebellion vs. sovereignty.

Remember, love covers a multitude of sins; so what shall we do? LOVE!

Problems do not have to ruin your life. They do not need to take you over or skew the purpose and direction of your call or your church. We all have the power to make the determination that we will not let the trivialities of life derail us from who we are in Christ and His purpose for us. Most conflict is trivial, but we are never to approach it as trivial. It is to be taken seriously so it can be resolved and the more important things in life can be pursued. Use this process to also learn more about the other person and yourself. Learn how to be better in your character and maturity and your relationship with God. See challenges as opportunities to learn and grow in His presence and His Fruit.

By following a few simple ideas from the precepts of His Word, we can save ourselves a lot of pain and hurt and drastically improve our relationships. Just by understanding the other person, you will do wonders for relationships and your church! The focus is what we talked about in the first chapter with Fullness and the Kingdom of God. The relationship is the priority, not the material goods or desires that may come up. When we are operating our lives in God's parameters, we are glorifying Him, building His Kingdom, and living in Fullness. When we are steeped in our pride, we are destroying our relationships and bringing shame to His Church. Why would we want to do that and take on all of the bitterness, resentment, hurt, and frustration in life, when we can have so much better?

Remember this very important fact; unresolved conflict costs much more than the cost to resolve it. In fact, to not manage conflict will enormously cost your relationships and church. It will cost you money, time, lost productivity, shattered relationships, lost children, dissolved marriages, bad decisions—and it can literally kill and destroy you and all that you know. It could have been turned around, but nobody wanted to bother with it! Do not let this happen to you, your friends, your family, or your church!

Therefore, as God's chosen people, holy and dearly loved, clothe yourselves with compassion, kindness, humility, gentleness and patience. Bear with each other and forgive one another if any of you has a grievance against someone. Forgive as the Lord forgave you. And over all these virtues put on love, which binds them all together in perfect unity. Let the peace of Christ rule in your hearts, since as members of one body you were called to peace. And be thankful. Let the message of Christ dwell among you richly as you teach and admonish one another with all wisdom through psalms, hymns, and songs from the Spirit, singing to God with gratitude in your hearts. And whatever you do, whether in word or deed, do it all in the name of the Lord Jesus, giving thanks to God the Father through him. Colossians 3:12-17

For more insights checkout our Leadership Cannel on the series on conflict "Problem Solving" at
www.churchleadership.org/

Section II

Using Small Groups to Plant a Church

Chapter 11

-->

Developing a House Church from your Small Group

If you want to plant a church, this is how; begin with a small group. Just about every church from Acts 1:14 through the Early Church, through today, were started from a small group or a smaller group sent off from another larger body.

Do you or your people struggle with role and placement in church? Do your people feel disconnected or lost in church? Do they feel like they are unimportant or not noticed or appreciated? Do they feel they are not getting fed spiritually or challenged to grow? Do they feel they have few opportunities to exercise their gifts and call? Do you feel called to plant a church? This chapter is for you...discover the purpose and role of a small home fellowship and how, through it, you can be better utilized for our Lord's glory! You can use your small group to plant one or multiply your church!

What is a "House Church?"

A House Church is a real, effectual, local, small congregation of Christians worshiping and practicing its faith. It can be in a middle class home in a US suburb, the basement of a church building, in a garage in an undisclosed country where it is illegal to have a church, or in the back of a business in a developing country. It is a house of worship, one that is as old as the Church itself. It is the archetype of the first intimate Christian gatherings and means that Christ used to form His Bride, the Church. It is the simple organization that fulfils His call and purpose for worship, discipleship, care, and fellowship. It is not a building; rather, it is a movement of people in Christ. A house church or a meta church or a home fellowship—whatever name you give it—is God's unfolding plan upon lives collectively as they come together to worship, fellowship, learn, serve, and inspire one another. I first helped plant a house church while in seminary; it was 1987 and a rather oddball thing to do. After a couple of years, I handed it over to a capable leader, and it want strong for many more years. I started another one in 1992, and we had a great four-year run. Then I did it again, as the song goes, *"Oops, I did it again"*, in 2001; we are called *Journey* and are still going strong. Our small home church is attached to a mega church in the LA area. This is where I tend to strut my so-called pastoral abilities to lead, learn, make mistakes, beta test our resources, and pray a lot. Most importantly, this is where we seek to glorify our Lord and Savior Jesus Christ!

> *Somehow, the art of church seems to have gotten lost as well as the reading of the Bible, for the most part, as faulty trends and misguided agendas have taken over.*

Many of us have forgotten what we are to do and why we are to do it. The house church is a means to remind us of God's call and purpose for any church fellowship—no matter how big or small. The word *church* in the Bible means "those who are called out." Also, *members of one body* from chapter three of Colossians is about the call to be closer to Christ. As a community, the closer we are to Christ our Lord the closer we can be to one another and to what Christ has called us to do and be. Once we make real peace with God, we will be able to make and maintain peace with others. In practice, this means we, as believers, are to be together and tighter, and we need each other to carry out our mutual faith. In addition, unity and peace among the fellowship and in the world are essential as displays for Christ, because we are His ambassadors. As examples of how God brings peace to all of us, we then are better able to really show others that they can have peace and salvation, too. If we fight and are in disharmony, or if we get distracted from the principle of a church, "how can God be of peace" will be the objection from those who do not know Him (whom we are called to reach) or are new to the faith (Rom. 12:4; 2 Cor. 5:20; Eph. 3:6; 4:24-26; Col. 3:15; 4:7-18).

What is the Difference between a regular Church and a House Church?

A house church, sometimes called a "cell church" or a "home fellowship" small group, is a more intimate and smaller gathering, usually six to fifty. A cell church is usually a small group from a church, and a home church is an actual full fledged church that meets in a home that may have higher numbers of worshipers. It is a group of committed Christians who come together as a community under a pastor or trained leader to worship Christ and follow His principles while meeting in someone's private home. It is less formal, has less bureaucracy, less institutionalization, but usually still needs to be connected to a larger body for resources, training, and supervision, as well as for accountability. The house churches I have pastored and seen tend to be more effective in building community, allowing a more casual atmosphere for people to invite friends who may not go to a "regular church." This also helps them be more mobile to better engage the surrounding community in friendly outreach (Acts 2:42; 19:25-41; 20:20; 1 Cor. 14:22-26; Col. 3:16; 4:15; Heb. 10:24-25; James 2:2).

> *A home fellowship made from your small group is still a church; it is just smaller and, usually, more agile and responsive. It is like the "light infantry" unit of an army that goes ahead of the regular attack force (a mechanized division or a full on rank-and-file army), because the unit carries less a load and can move faster.*

It is a tool of God to use us better in community. It is a platform to proclaim the Good News of Christ, to share the Gospel. This means "God delivers" and salvation is from, and only from, God, Christ as Lord. This refers to the person and Work of Christ, how He delivered us out of sin and into new life. It is by His life and sacrifice that we have the Kingdom and abundance of life here and forevermore. As a house church becomes too big, it can have a "good split" and have two, then four, and so forth. It becomes an example of multiplying networks and energizing and influencing more people for the Lord. The key factor that makes this work is prayer and is fueled by our gratitude for Christ, translating into excitement. Being excited about who you are in Christ is an essential aspect of attracting people and motivating them for and in leadership. New Christians bring in most of the new converts because they are excited and are energized. Even though new Christians may be ignorant on theological and apologetical matters, they are bringing people in versus people who have been Christians for many years who tend to lose their excitement and, thus, may rarely bring people into the church. A house church helps build excitement (Heb. 2:3).

After nearly two thousand years of the Church, we often need a reminder that we are all a part of the body of Christ, in community with one another and in unity with Christ for His work. Our faith needs to be grown and exercised; the smaller church cell or a smaller group in a bigger church becomes an intimate platform of great value to us. Christianity is not to be a spectator sport; it must be engaged with our best means for God's glory for all things in our lives—school, work, family, ministry, and relating to strangers. It must all glorify our Lord! This gives comfort, taking mere encouragement and putting us, as a community, into closer and more effective action. It is not just saying to someone, "do well," but helping him or her to do it. And, we can take comfort in that even though we are small, we are never alone, never away from God or from one another, unless we isolate ourselves, as these early church folks, that Paul writes about in Colossians, were seeking to do (Psalm 2:8; 22:27-31; Isa. 9:5-6; Matt. 28:19-20; Acts 2:39; Rom. 11:16; 15:9-12; 1 Cor. 1:2; 7:14; 12:13; Col. 3-4; Heb. 4:1-11; 10:19-25; Rev. 7:9).

The House Church restores what Communion was meant to be.

We can be better able to partake and celebrate the Lord's Supper and remember what our Lord did on our behalf. The debate that rages amongst most denominations and theologians are whether Christ is actually the elements of bread and wine or His role in it. However, what is usually left out is what it is supposed to be about. The original Communion and what the Church practiced for over three hundred years was fellowship and remembrance of our Lord that took place during a meal. This meal was not a tasteless prefab wafer and a shot glass of juice; it was real food and fellowship together that was practiced correctly as a gathering in private homes. Over time, it evolved into traditions and as a part of the Sunday worship of the local church. The Lord's Supper also pointed toward consummation of the Kingdom of God and a church is the practice of this; we show Him in and by our fellowship and worship (Luke 22:20; Matt. 26:26-28; John 17:21-24; Rom. 5:5; 1 Cor. 10:14-17; 11:17-26; Eph. 2:5-6).

Jesus had two suppers with them; one was a meal and the other was to commence a lasting ordinance, a sacrament to remember and honor Him (not a part of our salvation; rather our response to Christ). We see the bread and the cup as a real intimate encounter with our Lord. In most churches, we tend to forget this; perhaps it has become just a ritual and rhetoric to many, or shortened for logistical reasons, but the real meaning is far more profound. We have a Savior who not only saved us, but demonstrated victory and character. Jesus models committed character--character that shows the works of the Spirit even in the midst of extreme and dire circumstances and His pending, agonizing death. Jesus' character was in contrast to the pious frauds who called themselves "religious leaders," who sought their own will and used their innate wickedness to destroy Him. Jesus submitted to the will of the Father, modeling for us submission, surrender, and poured-out obedience to Him, and this is what we practice, model, and teach as a fully engaged church (Luke 22:17-20).

As *Jesus took bread*, we are to partake upon Him, as it was the custom of the head of the household to give thanks and a blessing before a meal; we can do so as a communal gathering in His Name. What was said was, "this is the bread of affliction our ancestors ate when they came out of Egypt." The bread now represents Jesus' body, given for all. Jesus represents the affliction, as He took our afflictions and sins, and bore (emptied) them on the cross for our eternal life. As the bread then represented the Jews being saved and brought out of Egypt, it now represents our being saved and brought out of our sins (Luke 22:19; Rom. 8:30; Eph. 1:5; 1 Cor. 1:30; 11:24).

As *Jesus took the cup*, a leader of a home fellowship takes the center cup and raises it, up to four times (as in four cups full), to pronounce blessings. This represented Jesus' blood, shed as a sacrifice to pay for our sins and judgment so God's wrath would "pass over." It represents His substitution and His sacrifice on the cross. We are gathered for worship and not for power or control; we can have the real substance that the cup represents, the real honor to trust and obey His commission and sacrament (2 Cor. 1:20; 4:13).

A house church can do a better job at communion, whereas a regular church can't because of logistics, time, and tradition. Thus, once a month or as led by the Lord, a home fellowship can share a meal and at the end, as Jesus did, have an informal communion celebration. (A small group or Bible study can do this too!) We can come for a meal that is shared together as Jesus established it on the night before His Crucifixion. After they had their supper and fellowship, Jesus told the Disciples that the cup of wine represented His own blood, shed to establish a new covenant between God and humanity. The bread represents His body broken on our behalf. Thus, when the Lord's Supper is partaken, we meet Christ and are made present with Him (Omnipresence of God) in remembrance of His atoning death and sacrifice on our behalf, and as it looks to the fullness of the Kingdom of God. As Calvin said, *"we are given a taste of Heaven"* and when we do this as a mealtime in a small fellowship together, we get a better picture and understanding of what a church is supposed to be (Isa. 52:15; 53:12; Matt. 26: 17- 46; Mark 14:22-25; Luke 22:15-20; John 6:37-39; 10:15-16; 1 Cor. 11:20-25; Eph. 1:13-14; 2:8).

God's Call for the House Church

Any church is about giving Christ the glory. It is not about you or me, the leaders or the place, or the traditions; it is about honoring, worshiping, and learning about our Lord. The Church universal and the church local is and must be all about Jesus Christ. We exist in and through Him; our relationship and our worship all must point to Him, whatever denomination we are, wherever we meet, whether we are in a magnificent cathedral that is a thousand years old or in a cold damp basement meeting for the first time (Jer. 7:23; 31:33; Psalm 73:24-28; Matt. 18:15-20; John 17:21-23; Rom. 11:36; 1 Cor. 10:31; 11:25; Gal. 6:1; Col. 1:18; 3:17; Heb. 8:7-13; 10:25)!

Francis Schaeffer stated many times—most notably in his book *The Church at the End of the Twentieth Century*—"that it is interesting, however, that the church was in the home." A "real true church" is not about buildings or even programs. It is a gathering with a purpose to know and grow in Christ, to spur on one another in the faith, to practice the "one anothers" in Scripture—that we are equipped and encouraged to grow and live out our faith in our personal lives and, collectively, in the world. In fact, if you study church history, there were no buildings for the first 300+ plus years. All churches were in homes and some were even underground to avoid persecution. They thrived and grew. When the church became an institution, the real trouble came—not from persecution but rather from pride, power plays, and lost focus. Traditions set in and Christ was so clouded by our ritual and the over-fixation of customs and religious practices that there was no effectual reason or function for the church except for power and control over people's lives. These are the real enemies of the Church. The church became lost in its own institution when it was once alive in the homes!

Today our churches can easily become lost and misguided by our institutions and traditions as well as our personal agendas, pride, and power plays. When the Church becomes over institutionalized, it becomes a blubbering bureaucracy. This can be good for resources and accountability, but bad for mobilization and response. We must be careful we do not lose what we are supposed to be about and do! The house church is not immune from these ills, but can be better at controlling the works of the flesh with a better focus on what the church is to be.

The House Church helps us Pay Attention

In Hebrews 10, the author addresses his readers and hearers (including himself) to say that we must pay attention to Christ with faith and hope. He is giving encouragement for an essential aspect of faith; it is trusting in Christ, but not blind faith, because we know in whom we trust. This gives us the assurance of Christ on whom we lean, learn, and model in our homes where people are invited to participate in His worship. We do not need to go to an altar or a priest since Christ fills that role Himself. Thus, as a home church, we look to Christ as the Priest, and we are the leaders and equippers to those who come; we always point to Him. Jesus now asks us to come, whereas earlier we had to stay away and give a sacrifice that was very temporary. In addition, if one's heart was not right, the sacrifice was not accepted. Now we can go before Him anytime and anywhere. In context, we are given four conditions: 1. *Sincere heart*; 2. *Undivided allegiance,* as in loyalty to Christ and His

Church; 3. *Full assurance of faith*; 4. *Hearts sprinkled and bodies washed.* The question is *Why do we not do this, or why do we do it so infrequently?* The point is this: *Are we filled with gratitude for who He is and what He has done?*

> *This is not a popular notion, but it is true: Christianity comes with a catch—an obligation or an entrance fee, so to speak. It is so simple, some people reject it; it is so difficult that others can't stand it. Yes, our grace is free without works or effort on our part; however, it requires our belief in Christ to receive Him and His work in our lives. That we see our need for Him, what our Lord did for us, and our responses to Him all comprise the Gospel Message. This is why we come together in fellowship to worship—in a large church or a small home church. Being a Christian and being a church are all about Christ. It is all about Who He is and what He has done. It is not about you or me, other than our response in faith and resonating His love by living a life of gratitude for Him, which is our rest of comfort now until the day when we enter His eternal rest. This has been promised to us, spoken by the prophets, written down in the Scriptures, and lived out by our Lord. This rest is not just about eternity; it is trusting in Him for our lives now, so that we are fruitful now. We live a life that has no worry or strife as our hope and life are working by and in Him. We can rest in Him now and in eternity! So, when we lead or pastor a church, home or otherwise, let us listen carefully to Christ, hear His voice, and obey His call and precepts!*

The House Church Helps us Worship

Worship is a covenant and call from our Lord to come before Him and meet with Him with reverence, gladness, and joy. This is about how we *draw near* and give God the recognition and admiration that He deserves. Praise is our motivation of an impassioned, changed heart, with an emotional and mindful exaltation of our gratitude for what God has done. It is a call to know Him intimately and express appreciation to Him with honor and thanksgiving as well as passion, sincerity, conviction, and in reverent fear and trembling. Worship is the aptitude, attitude, and practice of expressing the desire to know our Lord and Savior further, and being grateful for who He Is and what He has done for us. Worship and praise are the giving of our best to Him. We do this because we are His; we give Him a heart that is already His. He has given His best to us already. In addition, we are enveloped in His eternal love and care for pure and useful purposes. This has nothing to do with musical prefaces or orders of worship. It is the matter of a changed heart that responds to Christ who is the audience of our worship, as we are the performers (Deut. 6:4-9; Psalm 24:4; 50; 65:13; 79:13; 95:6-7; 100; 150; Matthew 4:10; 2:2,11; 14:33; John 4:23; 9:35-38; Col 2:9; 3:17; Heb. 1:6; Rev. 4).

It is important for us to understand that the structure of the church is not as important as the attitude of our hearts and what we are seeking and responding to be and do! A church is a body of believers and does not need a building, but a building can be put to good use if used wisely. A body of believers does not need a campus, but one can be utilized for functions, programs, and activities. We have to realize that it is not about the church building or the pastors and priests, what we have done before, or what we want to do now or in the future. It is about Christ our High Priest who makes us the Church—not the buildings. Our holy places are where Christ resides in our hearts and works in our lives individually and collectively. We need a structure to facilitate this, but it can come in any form. Any structure that is reasonable and biblical can be an instrument of praise and glory for our Lord. On the other hand, it can also be a determent to the Kingdom. It is what we do with it that echoes His character and call. The house church can just be a more flexible and agile organization that helps form better community for allocating resource and passion for the Kingdom.

Do not be stuck on structure or traditions; rather, be stuck and trended on Christ!

Chapter 12

→

The Servanthood of the Home Church

Developing a House Church out of Small Groups

We are called to preach the Gospel not lose it in some institution. We are called to proclaim the Word, to read the Bible in our services--not hide it and our Lord!

We Christians, as the Church, are called to serve and to help one another in our "personal business" of life. This extends especially to strangers in our home, because our home is now also a church, and we may not know the people who come (be smart, be discerning, and have boundaries to keep your family safe) to glorify God and because we do not know what help we may need ourselves. This is not being intrusive or nosy, or allowing abuse from people; however, we are to be helpful when needed, in community and co-operation. This is what a home church fellowship helps us do. Many people, especially we pastors, often forget those who contribute to the ministry or who can be involved in it. We focus on the nosy wheel or what we plainly see in front of us and not see all the rest and their potential. This is not necessarily out of callous disregard, but out of our hurriedness of the moment, our focusing on our needs and ourselves over the needs of others. Paul, in his Epistles, cuts across cultural barriers and arrogance, and commends publicly, acknowledging many. We should be careful to always be people who honor and acknowledge others (Rom. 16:1-5).

> *Thus, when we came together in someone's living room for church, we can be better trained and unutilized for service. We can realize we are important and needed.*

Take a look at the word *servant* in Romans and other places in the New Testament: it means a servant who waits on tables versus a slave, who is usually called a *bondservant*. This is where we get our word for Deacon. As a home church, we all become deacons, like a Special Forces unit of an army, better trained and enabled to move and to serve (Acts 6:1-6; Rom. 12:7; Phil. 1:1; 1 Tim. 2:8-3:13; 4:6).

A Home Church Reflects our Responsibility to Christ

We have a responsibility to Christ! In 1 Peter 2: 13-17, we are given a template on how we are to respond to government, but it also can apply to how we are to be loyal and serve in the church. We are called to do what we do *for the Lord's sake;* this is about authority. God establishes and *is* the authority. For this reason, Christ is extolled; His name and reputation remain good and shown in good light because we are His windows to the world! When we are submitting to others, we are submitting and serving as Christ did for us—and He is Lord! When we disobey Him or other authorities to get our way, we are disobeying God who opened the homes of those people in their leadership positions. We are to show respect. We Christians are to obey as long as our obedience does not contradict our obedience to the Lord and His precepts. We are never to violate the law of God, and this mindset will help set the tone for communion and fellowship in a small home church (Prov. 16:10; 21:1; Matt. 22:21; Acts 4:19; 5:29; Rom. 13:1-7; Col. 3:23-24).

> *Our responsibility and service help us worship our Lord with Praise, and in context, this also means being respectful and servant-orientated to others with thankfulness.*

Our response to God and to others sets the atmosphere and ambiance that resonates in the home church and that attracts others to us. This is more important in a home fellowship because it is also someone's home, someone's hospitality, and we can't hide from one another like in a regular church. We can't say one thing and do another to hide our true identity as a Christian, or to act outside of God's call and virtue. It also disproves the erroneous idea that because we have grace, we have a license to sin and to usurp our will over others. In this historical context, Christians are cautioned not to use the excuse of liberty to violently rebel against Rome (1 Cor. 7:20-24; Gal. 5:13; 2 Pet. 2:19-20).

To help ourselves, we need to see how we are to be as the *Will of God*, with every and all due respect to God's sovereignty. **He is** in control, and He places us where we need to be for His glory. We are called not to abandon our responsibilities and duties, because Christ, as our ultimate Master, is the one we obey, respect, and worship (Rom. 1:1; 6:22; 9:3; 1 Cor. 15:3-8; James 1:1). A *bondservant* was the lowest form of a slave in Greek times, totally at the master's disposal, and even expendable. He, along with others like him, rowed the boats of war with a whip at his back. For us, "bondservant" means total, surrendered devotion to the Lord; our will has been sacrificed to God's will and thus we are totally at the disposal of our Lord. We are not slaves in the social sense, but we are submissive and humble and rush to serve—not hide and be apathetic or conversely "lord it" over others (Acts 6:1-6; Rom. 12:7; Gal. 1:15; 2:20; Phil. 1:1; 1 Tim. 2:8-3:13; 4:6)!

In Peter's Epistle, the background was that Christianity was getting a bad reputation from rumors and false allegations and was being expounded by the bad actions of some Christians. This affected the church that met in people's homes. When servanthood was forgotten, pride stepped in and took over. The church was at a crossroads between dysfunction and the true worship of our Lord. When we are good Christians, and when we are behaving with good character, we prove Christ. When we act foolishly, we prove our accusers right. This is an important call and is instrumental in countering false accusations and persecution; it also shows a better picture of the Gospel to unbelievers!

A Home Church Reflects our Responsibility of Servanthood to Christ

We are called to recognize and respect those in authority (Ex. 22:28; 1 Kings 21:10; Prov. 24:21). We are also called to recognize and respect the significance and value of the personhood of all people—regardless of race, color, or creed (Prov. 1:7; 8:13; 16:6; Rom. 2:11; James 2:1.)! As human beings, we are all the same, and we bear the image of God (Gen. 1:27; 6:9; 1 Pet. 1:17)! This helps when we are giving reverence to God as Lord, not as an afterthought or when it is convenient. We are to come before God in this way, along with humbleness (1 Pet. 5:6). We become an instrument of endearment and respect that is supercharged with more meaning and power because of our intense reverence and awe of God and His holiness (Job 28:28; Prov. 1:7; 3:5; 8:13; 9:10; 16:6; 31:30; Psalm 2:11; 34:11; 111:10; Isa. 12:6; Eccl. 12: 13; Mal. 1:14; Matt. 10: 27-33; Rom. 2:11; James 2:1). It does not mean we are afraid of Him; rather, we are fearful of His wrath (Romans 3).

> *Why? It is about respecting Christ and His order and the structure He gives us for the greater good of all people. Otherwise, things would be worse and anarchy would result. Then, as soon as a home church was set up, it would close down. This understanding of servanthood helps quench personality clashes, motivates unity, receives vision, and readies us for mobilization.*

When we model goodness, it is convicting and inviting. Misdirected people and even leaders may get the message that their prideful ways are not so good. We all need examples of character and virtue, especially when we do not have it or have never experienced it. This is essential in a family home and when that home hosts a church. God is the One who appoints leaders. Leaders will be held accountable for their ways, whether good or evil; we are to remain faithful to God and show our love for Him by being respectful to others around us. They will see His love in us, for love *does* drive out fear (1 John 4:18). Foolishness and the misdirection of authorities will be more thwarted by good examples than by terrorist hostilities (Rom. 13:1-7). By being the good example, and by ethics, we Christians can prove our Lord and make our homes an inviting and triumphant church. By remaining good examples, we show support for one another even in persecution!

No One in the Lord is Unimportant!

This is especially true in a home church, because each of its people is needed and wanted. One of the great aspects of a smaller church or a home fellowship is to help us realize the importance of interpersonal relationships, of cooperation—working together for a unified vision and purpose—and the value of encouragement! Our human tendencies are to focus on the big names, those in the limelight, and not realize the scores of people who do the tough work. Just watch movie credits and the hundreds of people it takes to make one, yet only the stars get the credit. So we think, "Hey, what can I do?" It becomes far too easy to hide in the church in which we are supposed to serve. In a home church, it is much harder to hide and a lot easier to step up and serve. We can better utilize our gifts and unity because we are all needed to serve. We cannot hide in the narthex and expect people to not see us, or worry we are not important enough to be used. It has been said that the service we give to others is the rent we give to live on this earth!

The total life transformation that Christ gives us will not only change us from the inside out, but will allow us to be an impact on others for the Kingdom. The question we have to ask ourselves is, *"What will our church do and be so that we can be the help and encouragement; will I be part of the answer?"* Will you?

The House Church Will Allow the Church to Persevere, No Matter What

Consider this: in countries where Christianity and a church are illegal for various reasons, Christians worship in underground house churches, and they thrive! The question to you is, *"Does your church thrive? If not, why?"*

God will persevere for His Church and, in Hebrews 10, calls us to persevere too—no matter what. While we are here on Earth, we can go before the Father in worship and prayer, boldly entering a reflection of Heaven before we go to Heaven. Each of us, as Christians, has the great privilege that the high priest in the Old Testament had only once a year. We have access to Him all the time. What is greater? It is all because of the blood of Christ shed on our behalf! This is what our new life in Christ is all about; this is what we are to do in prayer and praise, learning and sharing as a local or a home church. Christ has opened up a world for us to enter where we could never have gone before, all because of what He did for us. We can go into the presence of the Most Holy God, trust Him, and have confidence in Him so we can lead our lives with pure hearts, forsaking evil desires because of His promise that has been given and kept. God is trustworthy, so we can be faith-worthy.

When we plant a home church, or continue with one, we have to realize that it is all about Christ! We have Christ's empowerment and His assurance for living. We can hold onto Christ tightly and not waver when times are bad or we can't see where we are or where we are going. As we are encouraged to persevere, we can encourage others to trust in Christ, have hope for living, and demonstrate endurance in life and/or in any opportunities or setbacks we face. We can love and have outbursts of love and worship instead of stress. When you gather as a church in a home, meet in fellowship with love and respect for one another; one day, Christ **will** come again, and He wants us to be ready by exercising faith and confidence in Him now (Heb. 10:19-25).

In the Bible we are often called brothers, a reminder that we are all a part of the body of Christ, in community with one another and in unity with Christ and His work.

Therefore, we are never alone, away from God, or away from one another (unless you isolate yourself, as these early church folks were seeking to do). This allows us to build upon one another and be encouraged to keep on. It gives us the *confidence*, so that we have the ability to be bold and go before God because He has saved us, renewed us, and empowered us. We do not earn or deserve this outpouring; it is a gift of love and grace. (Heb. 2:1-4; 4:15).

The House Church is Still the Holy Place of God

When we do church, we are not merely entering someone's living room or basement; rather, we *enter the Most Holy Place,* meaning we have access to God's Heavenly Temple where before, in the earthly copy, only the high priests had access, and only once a year. We can never trivialize or condescend that a home fellowship is not a real church, because it is; when believes gather, it is a church--period. This is a monumental opportunity and shows us the depth and magnitude of how much we have been saved. We come together under the covering of the *Blood of Jesus*. We partake in His sacrificial death and resurrection—He who appeased the wrath of God for us. Because He did this, we can receive salvation, as well as the joy and honor of receiving forgiveness for our sins. God was more merciful with us than we could ever have been with anyone else or could ever deserve. No matter what we go through from persecution or loss, we could never catch even a glimpse of what Christ gave to us through grace. If we do not get this, we do not get church, and we will just fool ourselves much like a dog that chases its tail (Matt. 5: 3-12; Rom. 5:9; Rev. 1:5-6)!

We come together as a home fellowship to be tighter with God and one another, because we are in the presence of God, just as the priests in the Old Testament were when they went into the Temple and passed behind the veil that hid God's presence from the people, because no one with sin could approach Him. The ark of His covenant was kept behind the veil. Jesus tore the veil so we could all approach God in an understandable and able manner. Jesus is the veil that was torn for us; His sacrifice tore open the way for us to enter into God's presence and to know and worship Him (Ex. 25:10-22; Lev 26:11-13; Num. 12:7; Duet 10:1-2; 2 Kings 25:8-10; Matt. 27:51; Mark 15:38; Heb. 3:6; 6: 13-20; 9:3, 23; 10:19-20; Rev. 3: 10-13; 4:6-8).

Christ is over all, as in "Lord of the house." In Jewish tradition, the eldest son took over the family estate and/or business; he was the sole or primary heir. Now, Christ is Heir of all things. God's house was not the Tabernacle or Temple; it was God's people and Christ, the Shepherd of us all—those who are His faithful, the faithful remnant of Israel, and then those who accepted Christ (Heb. 3:1-6; Heb 10:19-25).

Our chief obligation as a home church is to help people worship, to help them *draw near*—partaking in an invitation to enter the presence of God. The church leader is to help lead fellow Christians in worship. Our example is our personal relationship with Christ. This means we have clear, uninhibited access to God because of Christ (Gen. 4:2-15; Psalm 15; 73:28; Jer. 30:18-22; Matt. 27:51; Rom. 5:1-2; Eph. 2:13-22; Heb. 4:16; 7:19-25; 12:28; 3:15-16; 1 Pet. 2:4-10).

Home Church can be Tough, Yet Very Rewarding

The closer we are to Christ, the closer we are to one another and to what Christ has called us to be and do. Once we make real peace with God, we will be able to make and maintain peace with others. In context, this means believers need to practice unity and peace among one another as a display of how God brings peace to all of us. If we fight and are in disharmony, we allow the objection--how can God be of peace--from those who do not know Him (whom we are called to reach) or are new to the faith. Paul experienced strife and then reconciliation—a model for us all (Rom. 12:4; Eph. 3:6; 4:24-26; Col. 3:15).

There is no better, faster track to a great spiritual life than simply working on our faith. To do this, we need one another; we cannot hide in a mega church, we cannot remain unplugged from a small group or Bible study and expect to be fed and grow. We cannot just sit on a pew for an hour or so a week and expect to be transformed. We need more; we need to feed upon His Word, we need to fuel our faith by our devotions, and we need one another to encourage, equip, and keep us accountable. I believe a home church is one of the best platforms for this. Sometimes, a bigger church is unable to feed individuals unless they plug the people into smaller groups and/or mentorships. A big church can be more effective as a collection of home fellowship groups that come together for convention on Sundays, or it can be just one small church. It was Christ who bore our sins and redeemed us; He is the reason we do church. Why would we hide from this or seek favor from an alternative that does nothing? The answer is that faith is a free gift, but we must practice it and do so mutually in due diligence to build and mature it. We can learn to put off our fears and to put on our Lord.

Some thoughts on leading a home fellowship to consider:

- How can your home fellowship be challenged to do more to continue and complete the ministry Christ has given you?

- How can your church be an instrument of love and servanthood, one that exhibits appreciation and faith and desires to do what it takes to put them in action?

- What do you think God wants you to do to help others move their faith forward? What do you need to do to go beyond the mindsets that hold you back? Remember: faith is not blind or reckless.

For a deeper and more radical transformation, look back on your church life, your relationships, and connections, comparing how you once were with how you are living in Him now. Has there been progress? If not, what must you personally do before you challenge others to go and do? A church needs to progress, not merely in numbers, but in the far more important realm—the spiritual formation and mobilization of its people! If you are not doing this, you are not doing church!

Chapter 13

---→

What is the Point of a House Church?

Why and how do we do our home church?

The point of any church is that we must heed God's call, His plan, purpose, and principles all associated as His children and representatives. Why? We belong to God, and our call is to trust in Him, not in traditions and what has come before. We are to seek Him and what is to come in life and in ministry and in His second coming. This world is a mere shadow of things to come; we are bound for Heaven where glory awaits us. So, how do we live now? With our eyes upon Christ! We must live lives that declare who Christ is by faith and lived-out deeds. We are to think about Jesus, and ponder His precepts and call so He is our life and our all-in-all (James 1:12-18; Rev. 2:10).

The house church can be a phenomenal platform to proclaim and apply the Gospel Message as we live out our mutual faith and respond to Christ with our gratitude and spiritual formation. To do this, we must always realize it is Christ whom we serve; He is why we serve others. We must think, study, and ponder how His principles are to affect and impact us, as He is Christ the Lord. We are to see Him, believe in Him, know Him, and love and obey Him so our entire lives and our living room church is infused in Him and His Way. Furthermore, we are called to make this happen by seeking His truth, His teachings, and to walk in His ways by trust. We are to do this with hope because He gives us the confidence to have courage and the empowerment of faith, all because of who we are in Christ (Rom. 12:1-2; Heb. 2:9; 12:1-2).

Hebrews 10:19-25: How to Be in Our Homes When We Are Also a Church

- We do our home church as *brothers*. This is a reminder that we are all a part of the body of Christ, in community with one another and in unity with Christ from His work. Therefore, we are never alone, away from God, or away from one another (unless we isolate ourselves, as these early church folks were seeking to do).

- We do our home church with *confidence*, meaning we have the ability to be bold and go before God because He has saved us, renewed us, and empowered us. We do not earn or deserve this outpouring; it is a gift of love and grace. (Heb. 2:1-4; 4:15).

- We do our home church when we *enter the Most Holy Place,* meaning we have access to God's Heavenly Temple where before, in the earthy copy, only the high priest had access, and then only once a year. This is a monumental opportunity and shows us the depth and magnitude of how much we have been saved.

- We do our home church by the *Blood of Jesus*. The sacrificial death and following resurrection of our Lord Jesus Christ appeased the wrath of God for us. Because He did this, we can receive salvation as well as the joy and honor of forgiveness for our sins. God was more merciful with us than we could ever be with anyone else, or could ever deserve. No matter what we go through from persecution or loss, we could never even catch a glimpse of all that Christ gave to us through grace (Matt. 5: 3-12; Rom. 5:9; Rev. 1:5-6)

- We do our home church *through the curtain*. This represents the presence of God and refers to the Temple and the veil that hid God's presence from the people, because no one with sin could approach Him. The ark of His covenant was kept behind the veil. Here, Jesus tears the veil so we can approach God in an understandable and able manner. In context, this is a metaphor—that Jesus is the veil that was torn for us, His body torn to open the way for us to enter into God's presence, and to know and worship Him. This is also further argument for how Jesus is superior to Moses and the Law (Ex. 25:10-22; Lev 26:11-13; Num. 12:7; Duet 10:1-2; 2 Kings 25:8-10; Matt. 27:51; Mark 15:38; Heb. 3:6; 6: 13-20; 9:3, 23; 10:19-20; Rev. 3: 10-13; 4:6-8).

- We do our home church because we are in *the house of God*. This is a contrast to Moses who was the "house," as in lineage of Law and Covenant. Now, Christ is over all, as in "Lord of the house." In Jewish tradition, the eldest son took over the family estate and/or business; he was the sole or primary heir. Here, Christ is Heir of all things. God's house was not the Tabernacle or Temple; it was God's people and Christ the Shepherd of us all: those who are His faithful, the faithful remnant of Israel, and those who accepted Christ (Heb. 3:1-6).

- We do our home church to *draw near* to God and others, meaning an invitation to enter the presence of God. For the Christian, it is worship and personal relationship with Christ. This means we have clear, uninhibited access to God because of Christ (Gen. 4:2-15; Psalm 15; 73:28; Jer. 30:18-22; Matt. 27:51; Rom. 5:1-2; Eph. 2:13-22; Heb. 4:16; 7:19-25; 12:28; 3:15-16; 1 Pet. 2:4-10).

- We do our home church with a *sincere/true heart*. We are to be dependable and faithful without ulterior motives to the practical applications and exhortations of Christ's precepts with a willingness to do them (Psalm 24:4; Jer. 24:7; Matt. 15:8).

- We do our home church with the *full assurance of faith*. This means that we are to have commitment; our faith does not hesitate because we are trusting in and following Christ. This sets us up for the coming chapter 11 and the *hall of fame* of faith—what godly people do with faith. Salvation is not for us just to be saved and sit in a pew; it is for us to be impacted so we can be an impact to others.

- We do our home church with our *hearts sprinkled*. This refers to the change and renewal of our hearts and minds when we receive Christ's work and gift of grace and are thusly released from a guilty conscience. This is about who Christ is and what He has done; this is about the freedom we have because of His once-for-all sacrifice (Rom. 1:8-15; 1 Cor. 11:4; Phil. 1:3; Col. 1:3; 1 Thess. 1:2; 2 Thess. 1:3; 2 Tim. 3:1; Philemon 4).

- We do our home church with *bodies washed*. This means a spiritual cleansing. Priests who went through the cleansing rituals could enter God's presence. We are cleansed before God's sight; what an animal sacrifice did in the OT law, Christ has done permanently for us, and we are washed so we can enter God's presence. (Ex. 24:8; 29:4; Lev. 16:4; Rom. 12:1-3; Heb. 9:13-14; 1 Pet. 1:2). This is now symbolized in our baptism as our initiation in our new life as we become identified in and with Christ by His work. In the Old Testament Law, this prepares us to worship God, for our sins are temporarily hidden. Now in Christ, we are cleansed by the new covenant (Ex. 30:19-21; Lev. 8:6; 14:7-9; Ezek. 36:25-29; Eph. 5:26).

- We do our home church as we *hold unswervingly to the hope* Christ has for us. This means having an unshakable confidence--without doubt or hesitation—in our trust in Christ. The reason is because Christ is faithful, even when our friends and circumstances are not. Our confidence is in Christ, not the people in the church or how we are tested or treated either inside or outside the church walls (Acts 21:26; Rom. 3:24-26; 2 Tim. 2:13; Heb. 3:1-14; 6:18-20).

- We do our home church to *spur* and *provoke one another*. We are to stimulate another in hope of Jesus, being encouragement. This is not just a spiritual gift; rather, we have a duty to do it, even when we do not feel like it. This is the support, using our spiritual gifts, all working as a team. This is the strength of the church; without it, we will fail. When we are discouraged, when we feel down—we are lifted up. The people with the gift of encouragement will be able to coordinate this; all Christians are able and called to do it. We are also to encourage people who are thinking of leaving the church to stay, and those who have left, to come back (Rom. 15:14; 1 Thess. 5:14; Eph. 4:15-16)!

- We do our home church *toward love.* We gather with and for the hope, faith, and love that are a triad of primary virtues from which character and Fruit flow out, by the work of the Holy Spirit. This is the foundation of the practice of the Christian life, our practical application and exhortation, and what it means to be transformed and renewed so we are changed and can be change agents in others' lives as well. Faith is also in community and mutual, as we each partake in Christ and need one another to grow further in our pilgrimage of Christian living. In so doing, we share Christ and therefore proclaim Him to those who do not know Him (1 Cor. 13; Col. 1:4-5; 1 Thess. 1:3; Heb. 3:7-19).

- We do our home church so we do *not give up* or *neglect meeting together.* We are not to give up or neglect or abandon the faith or the fellowship. This means having "concord,"; we are better together than separate. In unity, we have harmony and strength; as individuals, we are on our own and weak. We are called and made to function as a community; our only foe is our own pride that leads to our own destruction (Prov. 6:9; Matt. 27:46; Rom. 9:14-29; 2 Cor. 4:9; 2 Tim 4:10-16; 1 Thess. 2:1; 2 Pet. 3:9; Rev. 2:1)!

- We do our home church to *encourage one another.* In Christ together, we can be confident, optimistic, and faithful, buoyed up by one another's faith, practicing prayer and using our gifts as a community. Having *perseverance* means having confidence in God so we trust Him in difficult situations, and still see and trust in His grace and love. This means having the resolve and determination not to be faint in our relationships or situations, so we will be able to persist in dealing with stress and can accomplish what God calls us to. When we do this together, we encourage one another. We can do this by being encouraging with Christ-like temperament (2 Chron. 32:1-8; Esther 7; Luke 16:22-31; 18:9; Acts 19:8-10; 26:19-23; Rom. 15:14-16; Gal. 6:9; Phil. 1:6; 12-14, 25; 2 Tim. 2:25; James 5:7-12).

- We do our home church by *approaching God* and *drawing near.* All this is about how and why we build our faith so when Christ does come back, we are prepared. Theories of end times do nothing to prepare us; only the buildup of our faith does (1 Thess. 5:2, 4; 2 Thess. 1:10; 2:2; Heb. 9:8; 12:26-27; 2 Pet. 3:10).

Jesus understands us and the ways and opportunities and obstacles of life and fellowship in a fallen world; He knows the temptations of sin and pride, what we feel, and how to praise God. He is sympathetic with our plight in life and is concerned what we do with all that we face. He is our example and the One upon whom we are to focus. Are you sensitive to Him? Do you pay close attention to the reality and veracity of Christ? To His Word and precepts? If not, how will you lead a church? What is in your way that could possibly be greater?

Chapter 14

A Manifesto for a House Church

For any church to be successful, big or small, in a cathedral or in a home, we have to have a correct vision and alignment, to know why and what we are doing and where we are going. The Scriptures are our map and the Holy Spirit is our guide. It is not by pride, position, or tradition that we lead; rather, it is our surrender to His Lordship by which we minister to one another. Hebrews chapter 3 gives us a template on doing a successful home church:

- **We come together as *Holy brothers* to profess and give attention our Lord.** The title of "Christian" at this time, meaning those who are sanctified by Christ was considered a profane word and was used by those who hated the people who followed Christ; later, it was picked up in a servant stance as the name for those who profess Christ as Lord. Here, it is designating the recipients of this letter and calling them to pay careful attention to what is being said (Acts 1:16; 1 Cor. 3:1; Heb. 3:12; 10:19).

- **We come together as people *who share* and partake of His blessings.** We belong to Christ, and in so doing, we can participate together with and in His blessings. It is also a call to hold on to Christ as LORD and to seek Him—as place Him first in all things and situations. This is an aspect of perseverance by our faith and confidence in Christ, as Moses had confidence in God as He used him to lead His people to the promise land.

- **We come together with a *Heavenly calling* to persevere in the faith and grow in Christ.** This helps us to focus on what is important—Christ and our inheritance and reward of heaven to come. This also denotes our invitation to salvation, which comes from heaven and leads us back to heaven. Our life on earth is a mere shadow to what is most important: Christ, His Kingdom, and Heaven to come (Heb. 9:15; 11:16).

- **We come together to *fix your thoughts on Jesus* so we can have more confidence and faith**. We are to "contemplate" and/or meditate, as to put our mind upon Christ and do so thoroughly so to increase our fidelity in Christ. This is also a call to eagerly trust Him, as who better can help us deal with life and the challenges we face. Thus, we are to pay attention to Christ and what He has taught in all things (Matt. 6:33).

- **We come together as *messengers* to know and make known our Lord as the Father who sent the Son** (Matt. 10:40; 15:24; Mark 9:37; Luke 9:48; John 4:34; 5:24, 30, 36-38; 6:38). Jesus was sent by God and faithfully completed His mission so that we can do ours. Thus, He is the supreme Apostle who then sends us as His ambassadors to lead others to Him (Mark 6:30; John 6:38; 20:21; 1 Cor. 1:1; Heb. 2:14-15; 4:3-9; 10: 5-10; 2 Cor. 5:20).

- **We come together under our *High priest* so we can have direct access to God, face to face**. This was also the role of Aaron and his lineage, who did so ceremonially to mediate man's sin and to please God by making atonement—a shadow to what Christ does for us permanently (Num. 12:8; Heb. 1:2,10).

- **We come together to *confess and profess* our "confession of faith,"** that we make a lasting pledge that transcends our will so as we are living a life that is bought by Christ, we will live for Christ by our words and our deeds through His Word and Spirit by faith and obedience (Rom.

12:1-3; 2 Cor. 9:13; 1 Tim. 6:12-13; Heb. 4:14; 10:23-25, 35-36).

- **We come together as *He was faithful* to be faithful stewards of His principles and Way.** In Judaism, this also pointed to the Sabbath rest we receive in eternity that is our reward. This Jewish prelude may also been messianic, pointing to the "salvation-rest" of Christ's redemption (Num. 12:7-8; 1 Chron. 17:4).

- **We come together because *Jesus has been found worthy*.** From Deuteronomy 18:15-18, Moses' faithfulness had no parallel; Jesus demonstrated His faithfulness as Moses and the text predicted. The question to us now is, "how do you demonstrate being authentic?"

- **We come together because Jesus Christ is the *Builder of a house*.** It is He who builds our house church. This is a statement showing Christ to be Divine and distinct from the Father. It is also a contrast of God's house and a mere building, and to say how foolish to think someone who was created is greater than the Creator. Jesus is the actual builder of the house of Israel and the Kingdom of God and our local home church too.

- **We come together as *a faithful servant in all God's house*.** Christ is the Servant leader to the universe and Church. He deserves our reverence, dignity, respect, and worship (Num. 12:7).

- **We come together as the *Faithful* who accept the truth of God by being submitted to Him.** This is the essence of obedience from our trust relationship with God as demonstrated by Moses and Jesus Christ.

- **We come together *Testifying* to God's holiness, His regulations**, and humanity's need for redemption and a Savior—who was Christ to come (John 5:46-47; Heb. 9:8-11, 24; 10:1).

- **We come together under *a son over God's house* by His lead**. Here, Christ is Heir of all things. God's house was not the Tabernacle or Temple; it was God's people and Christ the Shepherd of us all: those who are His faithful, the faithful remnant of Israel, and then those who accepted Christ (Heb. 10:21).

- **When come together, *we are his house*.** The house is God's people, The Church, which is made up of the people who profess Christ and live faithful lives (1 Sam. 2:35; 2 Sam. 7:16; Eph. 2:19-22; 1 Tim. 3:15; 1 Pet. 2:5).

- **We come together as to *hold on to* and *hold fast*, because we belong to God.** Then we can respond to God by living by faith and trust in Christ. Our faith proves what He has done in us. When we persevere through life, we show Christ to the world (Psalm 95; Heb. 6:11; 10:23).

- **We come together as *instruments of courage and the hope*.** Determination of faith is the characteristic of a faithful child of God. This is a call to persevere, which reveals the depth of our character and trust in our Lord. If we do not come through trials stronger in Him and a better use for others, something is very wrong in our spiritual lives and our thinking process. Like the Parable of the Sower, our faith did not take root and the wind blew us away perhaps because we were never Christians in the first place (Matt. 13: 24-43).

- **We come together to *boast* and *rejoice* in our Christian life** because we have hope, wonder, excitement, and contentment. He is our all in all so we can have the confidence and distinction to *be glad in it* (1 Chronicles 16:10-11; Psalm 16:11; 37:4; 92:2-3; 97:1; 118:24; Matt. 5:12; John 10:10; 15:11; 16:33).

The home church is about Holy living, but it is not forced upon us. We are not adhering to a religion or a denomination, but a relationship with our Lord!

Holy living comes from a life that is transformed and renewed by what Christ has done for us! We can't mature in the faith when we punish ourselves, hiding in a big church and never being fed or else, skipping any church all together, or seeking some mystic or special revelations. Rather, it is knowing, trusting, and obeying Christ as LORD. When we realize Who He is and what He has done for us, we are then better able to respond back to Him and to others in gratitude, trust, and obedience. The original hearers of this manifesto had a skewed idea of God's purity and our sinful nature; they had it half right, that God is pure and we are sin. However, the application that *we can do as we please since we are in Christ* is purely wrong, especially in our churches. This now becomes a form of *relativism*. Such thinking and behavior equates a life and a church that is meaningless and produces little to no fruit.

Please see our small group channel on our websites for resources on how to plant and promote and utilize a home church. The basic ideas are transferable, the only difference of note is that home churches are larger and more church elements are incorporated, such as worship and sacraments.

Chapter 15

House Church Ideas

Being "Souled Out" for Christ to Build a Better Home Church

Principle Scriptural Guidelines: Matthew 7: 7-12; Mark 12:28-31, 33; Acts 2:42-47; 20:20; Romans 13:8-10; Galatians 5:14-22

> *The Call for a good Cell Church is Simple: to follow the Will of God and His Precepts and Glorify Him in all Things that we do!*

> *You shall love the Lord your God with all your heart, and all your soul, and with all your mind. This is the greatest and first commandment. And the second is like it, You shall love your neighbor as your self.* Mark 12:30-31

What is a Home or Cell Church?

There are two main ideas. One, a network of home fellowships that operate as a church by multiple 'cell' churches. Then there is the small group that grows and instead of dividing, it becomes a church either as a part of a larger one or on its own. Either idea, it a small group meeting as a small church. It is placing the majority, all who will go, into small groups with trained and equipped leaders who operate in the Fruit of the

Spirit for worship, biblical instruction, fellowship, prayer, encouragement, and ministry. This can be a standalone small church or a network of cells interconnected where the Sunday service is the weekly convention to praise and worship Christ the Lord and be further taught from the Word. Small groups can be the primary structure, care, and teaching machines in a growing healthy church, but only if it is focused on Christ and His Word and not on faulty and ever changing trends!

The Positive: Small groups are essential, and every Christian should be involved in one! This is a great model for knowing and growing in Christ! We can dig out an abundance of good stuff here and implement it for Christ's glory.

The Negative: Many of the popular writers and visionaries on this are losing sight of the main thing--Christ! Some of the emerging paradigms on this focus on unbiblical rhetoric such as *humanistic philosophy,* Word of Faith, Positive Confession, and Third Wave:

- Seeking signs and wonders without the substance of Christ
- Emptying minds for prayer instead of filling it with Scripture and Spirit
- Downplaying the authority of Scripture or watering down the sermon instead of preaching Christ and His precepts
- Focusing on false doctrines and disregarding the historic Reformation and biblical Christianity
- Making God into a cosmic bellhop and not surrendering to His Lordship!

Such things miss the point and even slap our Lord in His face, seeking trends in the business community and modern social sciences or misguided research rather than the Word of God. This will be a fatal error to your spiritual growth and your church. This de-emphasizes biblical theology which leads to faulty spiritual growth and thus, discipleship and essential doctrine is left out and brings in a filling of fluff that emphasizes subjective experience and meeting "felt-needs" instead of our real need to know and grow in Christ and make Him truly known by our transformed lives. Do not to this to our Loving Lord and His Church; rather be a "Fruitful Bride." (For more, see my uncle's book, *True Spirituality!*)

Another problem in this cell church model is poor leadership. Unless the leaders are adequately trained, and good teaching and curriculum are used, the groups will become social in nature, and no real discipleship will result. Effective care and ministry will not happen. This model also over-emphasizes small groups to the detriment of other areas, such as other essential ministries and calls of the church.

Essence of a Healthy Cell Church

The cell is not to be independent—rather interdependent, in Christ and then in one another. It is basically a more intimate structure that can be a small church or a network of many cells to make a larger church or a larger church more effective.

- Focused on Jesus over all else!
- Focused on the Bible, not Personalities
- Focused on Discipleship and Spiritual Growth
- Developing Positive Relationships
- Empowering People for Life
- Participation in Ministry
- Developing Leaders
- Outreach and Missions
- Multiplication
- Networking with other Cells

As with developing any healthy church, this is about seeking and applying biblical principles rather than just models for ministry:

- Christ rather than Inclinations
- Biblical Principles rather than Trendy Models
- Life in Christ rather than Methods
- Godly Goals rather than Techniques
- Essence of Discipleship rather than Systems of Structure

The basic philosophy of the Cell Church is the priesthood of all believers:

- The people are not to be "pew-sitters;" they are to be trained and empowered to participate and lead in the ministry and the lives of one another.

- The Pastor is the equipper and trainer, not the one to do the entire ministry; rather, he is to be the "asset to assist" others to do it.
- Equipping and empowering are the foundations that rest on Christ and His Word
- People are not just being trained; they are being empowered by the Holy Spirit and encouragement and instruction from the pastors and leaders--trusted to be released.

The basic heart of the Cell Church is everyone actively growing in Christ, serving Christ by reaching the lost, and seeing the reproduction of their faith. Here are some "buzz words" that facilitate this:

- Growing
- Developing
- Motivating
- Supporting
- Leading
- Offering
- Equipping
- Validating
- Adaptability
- Servant Leadership
- Appreciating
- Empowering
- Mentoring
- Coaching
- Delegating
- Multiplying
- Reaching

Here is an acronym to put it in perspective: LOVE

To Love and Care with passion and conviction for the people that God brings us, for us to be the people of God so we can do the work of God, and that we are growing and, in turn, helping others grow!

- **Lead** the people of your church to faith in Christ and the furtherance of their faith: 1 John 3:7, *"Dear children do not let anyone lead you astray"*. Let this be our first principle.

- **Offer** the path for spiritual growth: Phil. 3:10, *"I want to know Christ and the power of His resurrection, and the fellowship of sharing..."* Our second principle.

- **Validate** personal relationships in one another: Gal 5:22, *"But The fruit of the Sprit is love, joy, peace, patience, kindness, goodness, faithfulness, gentleness, and self control."* Our Third Principle.

- **Equip** Believers to grow in and serve God in purpose and call here and in the world: Eph 1:9-10, *"And He made known the mystery of His will."* For us to seek God's purpose to be our <u>every</u> principle!

Our LORD powers us to exist and to make Him known to one another and non-believers with the life-changing message of JESUS CHRIST. To mature the Believers in their faith, so they can go and do the ministry, and so they can be the disciples to the non-believers to the LORD....and so it goes....

Be "Souled Out" to God, that we do all things to the glory of Christ our LORD (Mark 12:28-31)!

- Souled Out is a mid-week Prayer, Accountability, and Bible study.
- Souled Out is a small group program.
- Souled Out is worshipping Christ our LORD.
- Souled Out is a Discipleship program.
- Souled Out is home-based rather than meeting at a church.
- Souled Out is an adventure to prepare others for life in Christ.
- Souled Out is an avenue for ministry.

To establish the groundwork of growing in Christ (Matthew 28:19-20):

BUILDING IN CHRIST

- Building a relationship with God daily.
- Denying yourself, putting Christ first.
- Serving God.
- Building relationships with others.

- Loving others as you love yourself.
- Sharing your life with others.

SERVING OTHERS

- Loving the lost .
- Building a relationship with the lost.
- Praying for the lost.
- Sharing with the lost.
- Serving the lost.

What Needs to take place to make a Cell Church:

- The primary role of the pastor and leadership is equipping the people.
- The goal is not to be a building or a collection of programs, rather a platform for spiritual growth and effective ministry for the Glory of Christ.
- The small groups will be a place for biblical instruction, accountability, nurture, and encouragement, as they provide the structure for spiritual growth.
- The discovery, development, and deployment of spiritual gifts.
- The need for a Spirit-filled life of service and witness.
- The motivation and mobilization of the laity to share the load and responsibility for the ministry of the kingdom of God.
- The emphasis is on relationships, first with God, then self (maturity and accountability), then others, and finally, the world.
- The children and youth are of extreme value and worth and a part of the church.
- The need to abandon any methods or trends that do not treat the person as a person in Christ
- The need to abandon any methods or trends that do not come from Scripture or are contrary to Scripture or that do not honor Christ.
- The leadership keeps tabs to offer help, reorganize potential problems, and problem-solves to maintain order and intimacy.

But the fruit of the Sprit is love, joy, peace, patience, kindness, goodness, faithfulness, gentleness, and self control.

This is also called the "Meta Church" (the biblical version). This was partially developed at the Fuller Institute in Pasadena, where I was on staff. I am one of its original researchers and founders. I took material from the Early Church and the Book of Acts, and also based this on *Serendipity*, *Son Life*, and *Campus Crusade* materials. The purpose was to seek a more effective and intimate way to embrace His Way through meta (small) churches.

Appendix 1

An *Effective Small Group Curriculum Model*

"Doing Life Together" we share, care, learn, and pray! This is condensed from Chapter 5 for 'handout' distribution.

This particular model is for a Bible based relational group, designed to build effective authentic relationships by engaging Scripture and life. Learn about them and from God's Word and apply His precepts to daily life. This type of group only needs this article, a Bible and selected verses for the study. A good one-volume commentary, a study Bible, and a Bible Dictionary can also be of help. And if you go through a Book of the Bible see the *Into Thy Word* website for study notes www.intothyword.org. Also, probable PDF's are also available of this and hundreds of other Bible Studies.

How to make this work best? Be willing to be a learner of life and the Word. See chapter 5 for more insights using this curriculum.

1. **Prayer**: Spend five minutes to open the session in prayer, Rev. 3:20!

2. **Read a short Bible Passage**. Start with the "one another" passages in Appendix 4. Or, go through Romans 12 with one or two verses at a time, or John 14 and 15, or, 1 John or James in the same way; use the passages from our Character series. Then ask the Essential *Inductive Questions* (for more inductive questions and curriculums on our Website www.intothyword.org see Inductive Bible Study Basics):

The Essential Inductive Questions

1. What does this passage say?

2. What does this passage mean?

3. What is God telling me?

4. How am I encouraged and strengthened?

5. Is there sin in my life for which confession and repentance is needed?

6. How can I be changed, so I can learn and grow?

7. What is in the way of these precepts affecting me? What is in the way of my listening to God?

8. How does this apply to me? What will I do about it?

9. What can I model and teach?

10. What does God want me to share with someone?

3. **Reflect**: How is God's Word impacting me, how can He impact me more?

4. **Listen** to one another. Ask how the past week has been.

5. **Questions** (Pick a few of these relational questions below and rotate the rest for each week.

- What has your week been like?
- Situations that you are dealing with?
- Good news?

- Bad news such as setbacks, failures, harm done to me, or what I have done to another?

- What is God doing in your life now?

    - How is He working?
    - What is preventing Him from working in you?
    - How is your Bible reading and study going?
    - How is Satan trying to work in your life?

- Accountability questions, choose one or two for each week see Appendix 2.

- Discus the assigned study, passage or devotional reading.

- What temptations/sins are you dealing with? What are you going to do to resolve them?

- Is there anything—issues, concerns, ideas you need to share or to confess to?

- How is your relationship with God? What do you need to do to improve it?

- How is your relationship with your spouse, friends, co-workers, and church members? What do you need to do to improve it?

    - Did you spend adequate time with family?
    - How is communication? How can you improve it?
    - What is negative in your family? What are you going to do to resolve it?
    - What is positive? What are you going to do to honor and reward it?
    - How are you maintaining your friends?
    - Were you hurt by them this week? How so? What can you learn? How can you bring healing?
    - What can you do to improve your relationships, first with immediate family, extended family, friends, coworkers, neighbors and then others around you?

- What is a longing in your heart, an issue or a person?

- What is your dream? If you could do anything, what would you do? What is holding you back? Is it in God's permissive will (not violating His precepts)? What do you need to do to make it so?

6. **Refocus** on God's principles. This is the time to listen to God and His Way. Go back to your study passage and ask some Inductive questions of yourself; keep it short and focus on "how can this passage change me?" Be willing to learn and obey.

Questions:

- Take an issue from the above, use good study notes, or a concordance or your Scripture knowledge (not pride or presumptions), and look up a passage to seek an answer from God's Word. A "Bible Promise Book" works great too; choose one promise for each meeting. You can also use the Scriptures and notes from our Character series (in the Character curriculum www.discipleshiptools.org).

- Based on what you have learned this week, what will you do differently now?

    1. What lessons did you learn?
    2. What mistakes will you now avoid?
    3. How can you learn obedience and trust in our Lord?

a. What is something good you have done or learned this week with which you can continue?

b. What Biblical application have you learned? How can this application or insight change you? How are you going to apply it? Benchmark a plan to implement it!

c. What Character is missing from or weak in your life that needs to be implemented or refreshed?

d. What is a bad character you have? What are you going to do to replace it with a good one?

e. How will you exercise the love and care from the Fruit of the Spirit to those around you this coming week?

f.   What do you need to do to better equip you this week?

g.   What are your eating and exercise habits? Remember, your body is the temple of the Holy Spirit!

h.   Are you confident in whom you are in Christ? How will this affect your actions this next week?

i.   Do you realize how much Christ loves you? How will this affect you this next week, and affect your relationships?

7.   **Resources,** how the group can help, what the resources are that are needed to help in this situation?

Questions

a.   Do you have any questions?

b.   Do you have an issue or habit with which you need help?

c.   What resources do you need to help you get over temptations?

d.   What resources in time, talent, and treasures do you have that can benefit someone in this group, church, and/or community?

e.   How can this group help with support, strength, skills, call, and encouragement for you this week?

f.   What suggestions or ways to help with a particular need do you have?

8.   **Return.** When will we meet again? How can the groups help one another during the day? How can we improve and grow in prayer, accountability, and accessibility?

a.   Did you connect with someone this last week?

1.   How so
2.   How did it go?

b. Do you need a call this week to remind you of something or to encourage you?

c. What can we do to enrich our meetings?

d. How do you need encouragement?

e. This is a good place to assign a passage, a study such as our character series, or a devotional reading for the following week. Agree upon it and keep it short and simple.

f. When and how can you encourage someone this week?

g. Who would you like to meet with this coming week?

h. Is there someone you would like to invite to this group?

i. When will we meet again?

9. **Prayer,** spend time fervently praying for each other and the issues from the above categories along with specifics that have come up!

Remember, you will only use a small portion of this curriculum each time you meet, keep track what you did and did not and need to do.

Appendix 2

Accountability Questions

Key passages: Proverbs 25:12; 27:17; Ecclesiastes 4:8-12; Romans 14: 13-23; 2 Corinthians 12:19-13:6; Galatians 6: 1-6; Colossians 3:16; Ephesians 4:9-13; 1 Thessalonians 5:14; James 5:15-16; Hebrews 3:13

Therefore confess your sins to each other and pray for each other so that you may be healed. The prayer of a righteous man is powerful and effective. -- James 5:15-16

Accountability allows us to be answerable to one another, with the focus on improving our key relationships with people such as our spouse, close friends, colleagues, coworkers, a boss, small group members, or a pastor. Accountability will also enhance our integrity, maturity, character relationships in general, and our growth in Christ. Accountability is sharing, in confidence, our heartfelt Christian sojourn in an atmosphere of trust so we can give an answer for what we do, see where we need help, understand our struggles and where we are weak, and be encouraged to stay on track, seek prayer, care, and support when we fail, and model guideposts for one another to keep us going.

Below are some key Accountability questions you can ask yourself and/or have a mentor ask you. These are designed for small groups and mentoring for those from high school youth to seasoned adults. They are for men's groups, women's groups, and so forth. Because of the number of questions, all you need to do is choose three or four questions for each week. If there is a particular struggle area, add that one, too. Also, incorporate one of the key passages above and spend significant time in prayer:

1. Did you spend significant time with God through His Word, prayer, quiet time, devotions, and other spiritual disciplines? How much; how constant? Is He your driving force?

2. What blocks your growth in Christ? What blocks growth, in your other relationships, from becoming more mature and effectual?

3. How has your time with God been? Did you pray for others? Are you satisfied with the time you spent with our Lord this week? How so? What can you do to improve it? Did you pray for the others in this group?

4. Have you faithfully served the Lord, His people, and the lost?

5. Did you go and participate in church activities and worship this week? How so? Why not?

6. Did you set spiritual goals this week? What were they? Did you achieve your spiritual goals?

7. Have you made your family a priority? What noteworthy activity or deed did you do for your spouse and/or family?

8. How have you struggled with sin? What are the sins that have weighed down your walk with God this week?

9. What did you do to enhance your relationship with your spouse/friends? What can you do to make that relationship better?

10. In what ways has God blessed you this week? How have you shared your blessings?

11. What disappointments did you face? Did they consume your thoughts? What did you do about it? What can you learn?

12. Have you filled the mandates of your call, work and school, practicing excellence, and being the best 100% as you can be for His glory?

13. Have you committed any sexual sin? Did you look at someone lustfully? Have you been alone in a compromising situation? Have you been flirtatious? Have you struggled with pornography or "romance novels?" Have you exposed yourself to any sexually oriented material? Did you put yourself in a situation with a member of the opposite sex that could appear to be compromising, even though it may not have been?

14. Have you shared your faith? In what ways? How can you improve? Have you had an opportunity to share with a non-Christian?

15. How well are you handling your finances right now? Have your financial dealings been questionable?

16. Have you been trustworthy? Have you lied? Stolen? Cheated? Been Dishonest or Manipulative? Have you elevated yourself over another for your own personal agenda? What about your language and attitude?

17. Have you allowed the media and its distortions in TV, music and movies to unduly influence you? What about peer pressure?

18. Have you been prideful? Have you been guilty of Gossip or Anger? Slandered? Shown Indifference? Been Greedy? Not Controlled your tongue? This hinders people from knowing and trusting Christ the most!

19. Have you demonstrated a servant's heart? How so? What have you done for someone else this week?

20. Did you struggle with a disappointment this week? How did you handle it?

21. Have you respected and treated your classmates, co-workers and peers graciously by showing them compassion and the love of God in your words and deeds? What can you do to enhance your relationships here?

22. How is your level of character, according to the comparison of Gal. 5:22-23 versus Gal. 5:19-21?

23. How did you practice *joy* this week? Have you had a thankful attitude toward God? Have you struggled with anger toward God? How so? What can you do about it?

24. Have you taken care of the temple of the Holy Spirit with rest, sleep, exercise, healthy eating, etc? What about addictions, gluttony, or substance abuse?

25. Has your thoughts been kept pure?

26. Are you giving to the Lord's work with your time, talent, and treasures? What about financially?

27. What do you need to do to improve your relationships with God and with others?

28. What do you see as your number one need or struggle for this next week?

29. Have you compromised your integrity in any way, or lied about the above questions?

30. How can this group help you?

Take it slow and easy. Don't try, or even expect, to immediately delve into the deepest, darkest corners of your life. Begin by having your close friends hold you accountable for things like praying regularly and integrity issues. As you see the benefit and results of this, you will also be building up trust, which is necessary for accountability in more personal and private areas.

If you need further help in this area, seek a qualified and trusted pastor or Christian counselor. Also, seek someone to whom you can be accountable. Do not just trust yourself; have a small group or mentor ask you these questions on a regular basis!

"When I kept silent, my bones wasted away through my groaning all day long" (Psalm 32:3).

If you fall away from these questions, or refuse to have someone hold you to them, Satan will have a foothold in your life. These questions are not just for the pastor or church leader; they are for all Christians who want to live a life of integrity and significance. The failure to have accountability will produce sin. At that point, it is not a question of *if* you may fall, but, rather, *when* you will engage in sin and destroy everything in your life. The relationships and ministry God has given you as well as your family and those around you, for generations to come, will be destroyed. Yes, there can be restitution and restoration, but the cost can never be completely repaid. Just look at King David; his sin had dire consequences with which we still live.

"The highest proof of true friendship is the intimacy that holds nothing back and admits the friend to share our inmost secrets." -- Andrew Murray

The Christian life offers glaring, empirical proof that "all of us make many mistakes," (James 3:2) and we are grateful for the forgiveness offered to us through Jesus Christ (1 John 2:1).

Appendix 3

Suggestions for Effective Group Prayer

On Building a Prayer Team: Important Qualities

* **Qualifications**: Commitment to Christ, one another, and Christ's work in the world (John 20:19-23; Romans 12:1-21).

* **Attitude**: View each other and all things through the eyes of Christ, with faith, hope, and love, (John 13:34-35).

* **Direction**: with Christ, under Scripture, by the Holy Spirit (Mt. 18:19-20).

* **Relationship**: Function as a team, members of Christ's body-open, honest, caring, serving (Romans 12:5, 1 Cor. 12:12-27).

* **Resource**: Almighty God, Father, Son, and Holy Spirit (Eph. 1:15-23, 3:14-21).

Getting Prayer Implemented:

1. **Form Group in circle.** For a short session of prayer, stand and join hands. This helps us 'form up' and concentrate. Try not to be scattered all over the place (One for all, (us together) and all for One (Jesus)).

   - We are going before the presence of God, and must do so with glad hearts and a wiliness to be together in unity and love.
   - We must never go before God in petty political power plays, jockeying for control or attention.
   - We need to be as a team, listening with care to others, with the same passion we have for our own requests. This is Christian community!
   - Christianity is not a solo endeavor, that God only has 'me' in mind; of course He loves and cares for you, and has you in His mind! He also loves and cares for others too, even those people you do not like!
   - It is best to keep groups under 10--4 to 8 works best. If you have too many people, break them down, and go to separate rooms if possible.

2. Each person needs to be ready and **eager to participate** (a passion for His presence).

   - We must not be in prayer when we have our hearts and minds pointed elsewhere.
   - We are to give God our best, which is our focused attention!

3. **Make one request at a time**, for effective concentration **just make 1** personal prayer concern at a time, introduced by 1 member at a time. Then all can be in prayer for that 1 item. As the request is given, others can best participate by listening in silent prayer. Then all join up in prayer, and afterwards repeat the process with the next request or item.

   - When we just blurt out a long laundry list of prayers they get forgotten and our minds are busy being focused on remembering them. Thus the prayer (s) lose out there passion and attention of us before God.
   - You do not have to stop the prayer, to get the next request. Make your petition in a state of prayer!

4. Make your **request uplifted** in audible prayer by at least by one (covered in love).

   - One person at least should speak, so it sets a tone for the rest in prayer; however, there is nothing wrong with just silent group prayer. Beware that silent prayer alone might cause a loss of focus and attention as people's minds will wonder.
   - Others may pick up from others their audible prayer, and restate it in their own words, or use it as a focal point for their silent prayer.
   - Do not all pray audibly all at once; it becomes disjointed and confusing (not to God, but to us, who need to keep focused). Remember God is a God of order, not disorder (I Cor. 14).
   - You can always add a word of amen, which means 'make it so', and gives your loving support. Amen does not mean it is over, the words of the prayer may stop, but not our attitudes and reverence to Christ.

5. **Wait in silence** before God until another member introduces a personal concern. Don't feel you always have to say something!

   - There is nothing wrong with silence. We must not allow it to distract us or cause us to be uncomfortable because the words of others may be silent; however, He is still there. God is the audience and the focal point of the prayer, not those beside you!

6. It is OK for each participant to pray as many times as they have concerns--but for only one request at a time!

   - Do not be in a rush! Listening is as important as speaking, in most case more important. Listening to others and to God!
   - Never, never, never, never use prayer to convey gossip!!!

7. Keep confidences in the prayer group, and do not bring details into the prayer that others have no business of knowing. God already knows!

8. Be sensitive and responsive to the leading of the Holy Spirit and the love of Christ!

Appendix 4

→

The *"One Another"* Passages

Bible passages essential for us to understand and develop healthy relationships by knowing we are called to *One Another*:

- Love one another: John 13:34-35; 15:12, 17; Romans 12:10; 13:8; 14:13; 1 Thessalonians 3:12; 4:9; 2 Thessalonians 1:3; 1 Peter 1:22; 1 John 3:11, 3:22; 4:8; 23; 4:7, 11-12; 2 John 1: 5
- Serve one another: Galatians 5:13; 21; Philippians 2:3; 1 Peter 4:9; 5:5
- Accept one another: Romans 15:7, 14
- Strengthen one another: Romans 14:19
- Help one another: Hebrews 3:13; 10:24
- Encourage one another: Romans 14:19; 15:14; Colossians 3:16; 1 Thessalonians 5:11; Hebrews 3:13; 10:24-25
- Care for one another: Galatians 6:2
- Forgive one another: Ephesians 4:32; Colossians 3:13
- Submit to one another: Ephesians 5:21; 1 Peter 5:5
- Commit to one another: 1 John 3:16
- Build trust with one another: 1 John 1:7
- Be devoted to one another: Romans 12:10
- Be patient with one another: Ephesians 4:2; Colossians 3:13
- Be interested in one another: Philippians 2:4
- Be accountable to one another: Ephesians 5:21

- Confess to one another: James 5:16
- Live in harmony with one another: Romans 12:16
- Do not be conceited to one another: Romans 13:8
- Do not pass judgment to one another: Romans 14:13; 15:7
- Do not slander one another: James 4:11
- Instruct one another: Romans 16:16
- Greet one another: Romans 16:16; 1 Corinthians 1:10; 2 Corinthians 13:12
- Admonish one another: Romans 5:14; Colossians 3:16
- Spur one another on toward love and good deeds: Hebrews 10:24
- Meet with one another: Hebrews 10:25
- Agree with one another: 1 Corinthians 16:20
- Be concerned for one another: Hebrews 10:24
- Be humble to one another in love: Ephesians 4:2
- Be compassionate to one another: Ephesians 4:32
- Do not be consumed by one another Galatians 5:14-15
- Do not anger one another: Galatians 5:26
- Do not lie to one another: Colossians 3:9
- Do not grumble to one another: James 5:9
- Give preference to one another: Romans 12:10
- Be at peace with one another: Romans 12:18
- Sing to one another: Ephesians 5:19
- Be of the same mind to one another: Romans 12:16; 15:5
- Comfort one another: 1 Thessalonians 4:18; 5:11
- Be kind to one another: Ephesians 4:32
- Live in peace with one another: 1 Thessalonians 5:13
- Carry one another's burdens: Galatians 6:2

Be devoted to one another in love. Honor one another above yourselves. Romans 12:10

Appendix 5

How to Build your Faith

The man without the Spirit does not accept the things that come from the Spirit of God, for they are foolishness to him, and he cannot understand them, because they are spiritually discerned. The spiritual man makes judgments about all things, but he himself is not subject to any man's judgment. 1 Corinthians 2:14-15

How to Develop a Devotional Time (this also makes a 2 to 3 week Small Groups study)

Draw closer to the heart of God by building a deeper relationship with God!

Peter talks about humbleness (2 Peter 1:5-7), which is characterized by the willingness to grow in Christ, by which we receive learning, resulting in the experience of rational, emotional, and spiritual growth. Two of the best ways to do this is through personal devotional time and by being a part of a small group Bible study. Peter tells us we ought to be humble toward one other so that we can know the Grace of God and not be in opposition to God. Secondly, he says we had better be humble, not only toward one another, but toward God. This is so straightforward. It is so essential to become a blessed and growing Christian and church, not necessarily in numbers, but in what is most important—discipleship—which is leaning on, learning from, and growing in Christ, leading to a lifestyle of worship!

How can I develop quality time with our Lord so I can become a deeper and more mature Christian?

Here are nine thoughts to get you pointed in the right direction:

1. **GOAL**: See where you are spiritually (Acts 22:8-10; Philippians 2:13) and determine where you need to go. Then, make a goal, and understand your GOAL. Your goal is to become complete, that is find fullness in Christ (Colossians 1: 28). To say it another way, it is to become a mature Christian, a person whose attitudes and actions are like Christ's (Ephesians 4: 13). Where are you spiritually and where do you need to go? Not only where do you want to go, but also where is God calling you to go?

2. **PROCESS:** Understand there is a process at work (Psalm 16:11; 73:28; Proverbs 16:9; Hebrews 11:1-6). It does not happen overnight, and you cannot get it in a bottle, off a shelf, or by sitting in a pew. The process is one of the main growth builders. It is about the journey as well as the destination. It is an essential step toward reaching your goal to spend personal, daily time with God. Thus, the journey is as important, if not more, than the destination, because in our walk, we are learning and growing. If we just arrived at the goal without the struggles of getting there, we would not have built any depth, strength, or maturity. Make sure your goals are a match to God's. We must never allow our presumptions and pride to cloud His way.

3. **PLAN:** Planning ahead (Isaiah 26:3; Mark 1:35) does not automatically happen. You need to plan out your devotions to make them more effective. You can get many prepared devotional schedules at a Christian bookstore or sit down on Sunday and decide exactly what paragraphs or chapters you will be studying during each of the next seven days. Doing this will eliminate the problem of spending half of your devotion time trying to decide what you will study that day. You can use a Bible reading chart, quality devotional books,

or a pre-written guide, but try not to just dive in. You will get much more out of your experience by having a plan.

4. **CONTENT:** Put into your devotional time variety and consistency (Psalm 16:8-11) in what you study. One month, you might study an Epistle. Then, you might spend a month or two in a narrative passage such as 1 Samuel. Then, you might go back to the New Testament to study a doctrinal passage such as Romans. Then, switch again to a minor prophet such as Joel. Try to go through the entire Bible in your devotional study within a year, or two years at the most. Do not stay in just one section, such as the Epistles, and do not skip the Old Testament, as you cannot understand the New without the Old. Do not use the same plan year after year. Break it up, and try new ones. Do the same with your devotional books. Mix them up. If you have a good one such as *My Utmost for His Highest*, by Oswald Chambers, stick with it for the entire year, go to another one, and then go back to Chambers in the following year. When we are too consistent, it may turn into rhetoric, and then you will have a habit, not time with Christ!

5. **FOCUS:** Set aside time each day by focusing on the purpose for your growth and maturity (Psalm 119:130; Isaiah 42:16; John 4: 23-24; 15), and then **make it a priority.** In doing so, you will be able to "go for it" with passion and vigor. Let Christ transform you through His Word. ATTITUDE is essential. You must start with the proper attitude. You are going before a Holy GOD! Usually, it is good to spend most of your devotional time closely examining a few verses, not rushing through multiple passages. This will help you keep focused. Some find it best to take notes and write down questions to ask a mentor about. In addition, you can set aside one day a week to switch from taking detailed notes on a few verses, to reading a chapter or two from a different passage without taking any notes. Whatever way you choose to go, stay focused and do not *bite off more than you can chew.*

6. **MATERIALS:** Get the best stuff you can get, and buy a good Bible (Ephesians 4:1-3) in an easily understood translation such as the *New Living Translation*. Consider using a Study Bible. I prefer *The Reformation Study Bible*. For serious study use the ESV (English Standard Version), NASB, NIV, or the

NKJV. The best devotional books are *My Utmost for His Highest* by Chambers, and *Evening by Evening* by Spurgeon. You can also get a notebook that can be used exclusively for things that pertain to your relationship to God and to other believers so you can write down what you learn and any questions you may have.

7. **PLACE OR LOCATION:** Select a quiet place (Luke 5:16) to study where you are free from distractions. Remove all distractions. Close the drapes, shut the door, turn off the TV and radio, clear all busy work from your desk, take the phone off the hook, and lock the cat in the bathroom—whatever it takes. You will then be better able to concentrate and have quality time with Him. Be serious about meeting God!

8. **TIME:** Select a quality time (Ephesians 2:18). Chose a time for your devotions when you are at your best. Usually, early morning is best, because outside distractions are at a minimum during this time. If you are not a morning person, do it when you are most alert. Give God your best. Set aside "x" number of minutes to study, and "y" number of minutes to pray. Be flexible to the Spirit's leading within this framework. If you have a short attention span (as I do), then break it up throughout the day. Perhaps read from the Old Testament in the morning, a passage from the New Testament at lunch, then read a devotion and practice intercessory prayer before bedtime. Remember, this time is holy, which means it is to be set apart to and for God only. If you are just being devoted to your plan and time, then there will be little room for Christ. The plan is the tool for growth, not the growth itself.

9. **SHARE** what you have learned (Psalm 55:14; Matthew 18:20; Romans 12; 2 Corinthians 12:18). We learn by doing and sharing. What we have been given is usually not meant for us solely; it is a gift that keeps on giving as we, in turn, help others. A willing heart, a teachable spirit, and the willingness and availability to share are essential for a disciple of our Lord!

From these nine precepts, we realize that from the character of Christ comes the conduct of Christ, if we choose to follow Him. Those values of our daily walk that drive our behaviors will, in turn, influence others and build our character.

You cannot lead where you have not been or when you do not know the direction to go. This is why discipleship is so essential to the aspect of being a Christian. We are called not just to visualize discipleship, but to do it—not just to talk about it, but to do it. One cannot just think about dinner and satisfy hunger. The ingredients need to be gathered, the meal has to be prepared. Only then is it eaten. The Christian who wants to go deeper and become more mature, as well as the effective church, will take Scripture and the call of our Lord seriously, and implement it and apply it to their lives.

APPLICATIONS: Here are some thoughts to consider about applying and turning your devotional time into action.

1. You will never be able to fully experience the value of a devotional time until you discipline yourself to apply what you have learned. Study with the determination that God will give you an application. Then, be willing and able to put it into action without fear or trepidation. Allow your trust in Christ be real and exercised!

2. Make your applications measurable. Think through the *who, what, where, when, how* and *why,* such as *I will begin showing more love to my neighbor by asking if there is anything I can pick up for them from the store next time I go shopping.*

3. Sometimes, you will see four or five specific ways the passage you have studied can be applied. It is better to select one you want to apply from the Word that day and do it. If you try to implement three or more ways, you will most likely get frustrated and fail. If you cannot decide, stick to the first one that pops up or one in the area where you need the most help.

4. Make most of your applications short-ranged, such as things you will do within the next day or so, or within the week. Periodically, God will give you an application that you will need to work on for a longer time. When that happens, rejoice and praise God, for this will build you up. At the same time, continue to work on fresh, short-range applications. See them as baby steps that will eventually turn into a marathon. Let God do a new work in you each day, and be thankful He wants to work in you.

When we are growing, we become contagious with the faith. We then are able to witness because we have something to say and something to model that people want. When we are growing, we will become the church that Christ designed, mobilized in Him to be welcoming and connective to others for Him. This is the church triumphant! Let us, as the church triumphant, pay heed to His call and follow it. Apply your faith. Then, watch your faith grow and become contagious to others!

Conclusion:

There are many ways we can do devotions and study the Bible effectively. There is no "best" way, only that we do it. Many Christians feel all they have to do for their spiritual growth is sit in a pew, turn on the television or radio, or naturally receive knowledge just by being a Christian. However, this is not the way to transform our lives. We can no better grow deeper in Christ without any effort as we could go to a grocery store, stand in the produce section, and become a cucumber. To be a mature and growing Christian, we must read and get into the Word of God ourselves. We do it through prayer, hard work, discipline, concentration, application, and even more **prayer!**

Take this to heart: Jesus never asked anyone to do anything without enabling them with the power to do it. Let this be your encouraging motive (Matthew 28:20)!

Remember, Christ loves you, and wants the best for you. His way is the best way, and we need to have Him and the perspective of eternity in mind, removing focus from our limited feelings and desires.

Discussion Questions:

1. How can I develop quality time with our Lord so I can become a deeper and more mature Christian?

2. Has your passion and zeal for witnessing grown or diminished over the years? What were the reasons?

3. Why would someone who is a Christian refuse to share the gift of salvation with others?

4. What causes bitterness in people? How does bitterness come into play when you witness?

5. When someone is antagonistic to you because of your faith, how do you feel? How do you react and respond? How should you?

6. Imagine you live in a country that is non-Christian, and where it is even against the law to be a Christian. How would you hold onto your faith and reliance upon the Lord? How would you witness? What would you do if you were persecuted?

7. What are the distinctions, character, and personality of a Christian who bases all his or her life, IT ALL, upon Christ, with full trust and assurance by faith and obedience? What would this do to evangelism efforts?

8. How would you define "self-imposed" righteousness? How would you define "obedience" to righteousness?

9. How do we get to be righteous? What is the key ingredient?

10. Some Jews, as well as people in general, do not feel they have the need for Christ; what can you do to show them the Light?

11. If you and your family had been Jews all of your lives and for many generations past, how do you think you would respond to Christ?

12. If you are able to change, and Paul, the "chief sinner," was able to change, how does this give hope to others and encourage you to be persevering in being a good witness?

13. Christians receive the gift of Grace, but do not give the gift to themselves. How does it make you feel to know that you cannot earn or buy God's most precious gift?

14. What has your church done, or could they do, to cause our Lord to weep?

15. God desires us to have "beautiful feet" (Romans 10:5-21) to bring the Good News! What can you do to keep your feet beautiful?

16. Evangelizing and discipling are the main goals of the church (Matthew 28:19-20) and what Christ has called us to do and be. In what ways do you and your church do this? How can you do it better?

17. From your experience, what are some of the misunderstandings about Christ and His Church that cause people to reject Him?

18. Despite Paul's passion and the willingness of God to gather His chicks, Israel rejected God anyway. Why did Paul keep persevering?

19. How can the fact that we are not responsible for the results of evangelism keep the fires of perseverance and zeal lit under you?

20. How can you keep yourself and others from being discouraged from witnessing or obeying Christ when it becomes difficult?

21. Take a close look at who in your life, at work, school, at the shoe store, or wherever has not confessed Jesus as Lord? How can you bring the message of the most precious Gospel to them?

22. What comes into your mind when you see the phrase, *Follow Me* (Christ)?

23. Jesus comes as the good Shepherd to rescue His lost sheep. How are you, or how could you be, comforted with this truth?

24. What are you focused on? Is it money, job, family, hobbies, food? How is your focus related to God's focus?

25. When you are putting your faith into practice, how do you feel when people reject you or treat you badly?

26. Paul was viciously and personally attacked—and, for

what? For spreading the true Gospel. Read how he responds in Galatians 1:10. How can you be further empowered to serve and witness, knowing that you are not responsible for how or why people respond to you?

27. What holds you back from embracing God's call to you?

28. How much does fear affect your motivation to be involved in a ministry?

29. If we become tied down with possessions and worldly concerns, we will miss His call to participate in the mission He has for us. What are your thoughts on this?

30. How can a Christian balance wealth with his or her call? When do wealth, possessions, jobs, or money (if you think you are not wealthy, think again-especially if you live in the US, where the poorest of the poor live five percent above the rest of the world) become hindrances, and even evil to what Christ calls us to do?

31. When you do outreach, most people will not listen or care; that is not your problem. What can you do to break away from feeling rejection, knowing that it will be difficult not take it personally, in order to be effective for the Kingdom?

32. How can you keep from being shocked when strangers and family friends no longer accept you because of Christ?

33. What is your church doing now about evangelism?

34. What should your church be doing now about evangelism?

35. What are you going to do about it?

"Therefore go and make disciples of all nations, baptizing them in the name of the Father and of the Son and of the Holy Spirit, and teaching them to obey everything I have commanded you. And surely I am with you always, to the very end of the age." Matthew 28:19-20

Some passages to consider on discipleship and mentoring which are not options, but a command: Proverbs 18:24; Matthew 7:18-

24; 10:1-42; 19:28-30; 28:16-20; Mark 1:1-5; 1:35 -2:12; Luke 9:23-25; 48; Luke 14:26-27; John. 8:31; 12:20-26; John 14; 15; 1 John: 5:3; Romans 12; 1 Corinthians 3:5-11; 12; Galatians 6:1-10; 2 Timothy 2:7; 1 Peter 3:15.

More tools on Discipleship are available at www.intothyword.org, www.withtheword.org and www.discipleshiptools.org

Appendix 6

How to Improve your Relationship Skills

Faithful to my Lord's commands, I still would chose the better part; Serve with careful Martha's hands And loving Mary's heart. John Wesley

Romans 12:1-3

1. **SPEAK TO PEOPLE.** There is nothing as nice as a cheerful word of greeting!

2. **SMILE AT PEOPLE.** It takes 72 muscles to frown--only 14 to smile. (Besides, you may be on 'Spy TV'.)

3. **CALL PEOPLE BY NAME**. The sweetest music to anyone's ear is the sound of one's own name!

4. **BE FRIENDLY AND HELPFUL**. If you would like to have friends, be friendly!

5. **BE CORDIAL.** Speak and act as if everything you do were a genuine pleasure! (If it is right and good, it really should be.)

6. **BE GENUINELY INTERESTED IN PEOPLE.** Empathy means involvement!

7. **BE GENEROUS WITH PRAISE** and cautious with criticism!

8. **BE CONSIDERATE WITH THE FEELINGS OF OTHERS.** It will be appreciated.

9. **BE THOUGHTFUL OF THE OPINIONS OF OTHERS.** There are three sides to controversy—yours, theirs, and the right one!

10. **BE ALERT TO GIVE SERVICE.** What counts most in life is who we are in Christ and, then, what we do for others!

Appendix 7

---→

How to Improve your Communication Skills

Instead, speaking the truth in love, we will grow to become in every respect the mature body of him who is the head, that is, Christ. Ephesians 4:15

Are you a good communicator?

Here is how you can find out. Take a careful look at this character, that God calls us too, from most precious Word by examining the passages below. Now ask yourself:

Proverbs 29:20; Matthew 21:22; Luke 8:18; Romans 12:10; Ephesians 4:15, 25-29; Colossians 3:5, 16, 4:6; 1 Timothy 4:12; James 1:19; 1 Peter 3

1. How do I exhibit good Communication in my daily life?
2. What can I do to develop a better willingness to pursue effective Communication?
3. What blocks good Communication skills from working and being exhibited in me?
4. How can I make Communication function better, stronger, and faster—even in times of uncertainly and stress?

Communicating productively is one of the most important skills in life. This will be essential for forming and keeping an effective small group. Effective communication is being willing to convey our honest thoughts, attitudes, feelings, and actions to others in a kind and active listening manner that reflects and glorifies Christ. This is the foundation of a successful marriage as well as a healthy church and an affirmative friendship. Without communication, a small group or any relationship in the church, the workplace, the home life, or anywhere can never effectively work.

If we are not willing to engage good communication skills our church and homes will be filled with inarticulate conversations, not or listening, not effectively ourselves to one another—many, many times each day. Preferably, we should desire to do this effectively, sincerely, and positively, but in most cases, the message sent is not always the message received by the other person, and rarely are the messages from the hearer and receiver identical.

Thus, good communication is a must—essential to the understanding of one another. However, although the goal of perfect communication is perhaps unattainable, that does not mean we should not seek to be effective, as all of our relationships and dealings in life will depend on it. The first thing we can do to be better communicators is to have the desire to be heard and to hear the other person fairly. We can do this when we are sincere, enthusiastic, refrain from over-talking, be truly open, and make eye contact. Open communication is the vital foundation for every relationship, from the workplace to friendships, and especially in marriage, where it is necessary in order to understand and help each other. Without it, one cannot see what is truly motivating the other, or what his or her ideas and intentions are. Nor can we commune, learn or grow our relationship effectively. When you have differing points of view—and you will have—be willing to talk and listen. Simply by listening, 99 percent of the problems in your small group and life will be resolved. When you have this down, you will be light-years ahead of the game in your friendships, marriage, workplace and church.

What Can I Do To Be A Better Communicator?

1. Be willing to be open and honest. Be willing to express

feelings about the other, and the desires, aspirations, and plans you see for yourself and for your partner. This will build communication and trust! If you cannot express yourself, then get help. Otherwise, it will only escalate from bad to worse. You cannot gain anything by lying or playing games!

2. Communication, as well as understanding and the willingness to work together to commune and solve problems must be a cornerstone of the relationship.

3. The care we give is usually more important than the words we say! Courtesy is contagious!

4. Show interest in others; be positive and sensitive, especially in a marriage. Do this by asking questions, listening to each other fully, and not dominating the conversation. When you see him or her again, remember the important details so you can bring up what was communicated before and ask how it is going, what you can do to help, and so forth.

5. Always communicate without blame; always show the love of Christ!

6. Seek first to understand what the other person is saying and make sure the other person feels understood; this inspires openness and trust.

7. Be sincere; saying what you mean and meaning what you say is the golden rule to effective and edifying communication.

8. You are only responsible for what you say and how you treat others; you are not responsible for what others say to you or how they treat you!

9. Be yourself; be genuine, honest and real. Do not pretend or be manipulative. Remember, integrity is imperative at all times!

10. When there are disagreements, explain your position with logical reasons for it. Do not jump to conclusions or be emotional or manipulative. Any good position will be open for comments, evaluation, criticism, and the opinions of others.

11. Make sure you hear the other's position correctly. If you are not sure, are confused, if it does not make sense, or it is

incongruent, ask questions for clarification. Compliment the other person's idea, whether you agree or not, and be courteous. When giving a critique, be constrictive, positive, true, and respectful.

12. Paraphrase back what they said for clarity. If you think there is a misunderstanding brewing, ask a question, "May I restate what I am hearing from you?"

13. Be aware of your body language. Make sure you are not giving off negative signals or have a callous or insensitive tone. Remember, you may be doing this and not even realize it.

14. The choice of our words and the tone of them will have dramatic effects as it greatly affects the meaning, interpretation, and distortion of the message. Choose your words and tone carefully through prayer with encouragement in mind! Remember that most people will not attribute the same meaning to the same words! Clarify what and how you say something!

15. Allow others to give you constructive feedback whether it is ideas, suggestions, critiques, or confrontation; incongruent or not, listen and be in prayer about what you can learn and improve about yourself.

16. Being defensive or condescending, name calling, labeling people, being prideful, and arrogance are listening, communication and relationship killers!

17. Having selective hearing, ignoring important other information and only willing to listen to what you want to hear will seriously hamper your relationships as well as ability to communicate.

18. Do not jump to conclusions or be judgmental or legalistic! Having assumptions about the other person that may or may not be true hinders listening and communication.

19. Not speaking or communicating clearly, or being dishonest so the other person cannot hear what you say will lead to others forming untrue assumptions to causing serious and detrimental misunderstandings.

20. Keep in mind that when a person's feelings are hurt, he or she will retaliate, not negotiate!

21. Do not overreact! Always, always ask for clarification!

22. Whether you are a pastor, doctor, lawyer, or a dogcatcher, keeping confidences is paramount!

23. Always be a learner; seek what you can learn from this person, from this situation, and from mistakes made by you or others.

To effectively listen, we need to give the other person our full attention. We must be willing to build the skills of empathetic and active listening. To do this, we first need to concentrate on quieting our own thoughts and concerns so we can hear theirs. We all have a natural, internal commentary going; try to shut it off until afterwards. This will help you engage the person and remember what he or she is saying.

1. If you want to interact effectively with and/or influence another person, you first need to understand them!

2. When talking to someone, develop rapport by demonstrating sincere interest in him or her; focus on him or her as a child of God by investing time. This should be the most important person in the room for you!

3. Be empathetic; consider how you would feel in their situation. Good listeners will be sensitive and show care by identifying and having compassion for the other person and not be disconnected or detached. Sometimes, it is necessary in professional type relationships to have set some boundaries when interacting with patients or colleagues. However, it is essential to show empathy and care.

4. Honor and hear others' thoughts and feelings; express positive feelings and feedback.

5. Listen to the words and try to determine the essence of those words. Keep in mind that what you think they are saying is not always what they are really saying, so ask

questions so to clarify and gather more information.

6. Do not jump to conclusions! Do not form your impressions by preconceptions, stereotyping, or generalizing.

Having a problem? Ask, *what can we do to solve this problem together? What are some steps you see that could resolve this issue?* If that does not work, place the issue on what the purpose of the Christian life is about, to worship and glorify Christ. *How can we develop a solution that glorifies our Lord* (Prov. 19:11; Matt. 18:15-17; Eph. 4:29)*?*

Remember that LISTENING IS ESSENTIAL for life and your small group! Good friend-makers are good listeners, good leaders are good listeners. Be the person who listens (John 8:47; James 1:19-25)!

Let the message of Christ dwell among you richly as you teach and admonish one another with all wisdom through psalms, hymns, and songs from the Spirit, singing to God with gratitude in your hearts. Colossians 3:16

Appendix 8

Helpful Links and Further Resources

Small groups are designed to meet the deepest relational and learning needs of the congregation. Small groups can help provide the framework for us be challenged to worship God with joy, passion and conviction, by learning who we are in Christ so we can develop the trusting faith in Jesus as Savior and LORD. We will be better able to build Christ-centered friendships, and then be equipping others to impact the world all for our Lord's Glory.

Small Group Curriculum

Into Thy Word Ministries offers hundreds of free Biblical based and effectual curriculums:

http://www.intothyword.org (Bible Studies)

http://www.discipleshiptools.org (Topical Studies)

Evangelism and Lighthouse Movements:

http://alphacourse.org

http://www.lighthousemovement.org

http://www.ccci.org

http://www.lighthousereport.com

http://www.namb.net/evangelism/prayer/lighthouses

http://www.hopeministries.org

http://www.harvestevan.org

http://www.lighthouseofprayer.org

http://www.jesusday.org

Resources on the web

Resources for a Bible Based Christian 12 Step Recovery

http://www.churchleadership.org/pages.asp?pageid=67284

http://www.discipleshiptools.org/pages.asp?pageid=65408

More for recovery:

http://www.raphacare.com

http://www.newlife.com

For materials and ideas:

http://www.lighthousemovement.org

http://smallgroups.com

http://www.serendipityhouse.com

http://www.neighborhoodbiblestudy.org

Myers Briggs

http://myersbriggs.org

Make sure you check out the small group articles, curriculums, Bible studies, and resources from *Into Thy Word*! www.intothyword.org

Appendix 9

---→

About *Into Thy Word* Ministries

Your word is a lamp to my feet and a light for my path.
Psalm 119: 105

Since 1978, Into Thy Word Ministries' vision is to provide Christians with the most effective tools and the most effectual means possible to better understand and apply God's Word to their lives. Our call is a dedication to teaching people all over the world how to study the Bible in a simple, clear, and concise way! Our passion is to glorify Christ (Colossians 1). Currently, we are training thousands of pastors and church leaders all around the world. We do this through seminars, missionary efforts overseas, church leadership consulting, curriculum development, and our interactive Website resources.

The missions' arm of *Into Thy Word* (*ITW*) was founded in 1988 at Richard's home church in Pasadena, California under Pastor Paul Cedar, who is the founder and Director of *Mission America*. *ITW* was an outgrowth from Richard's seminar on "How to Do Inductive Bible Study." There are currently over 3,500 *ITW* associates who personally distribute our Discipleship Tools and curricula in over 80 countries through CDs, booklets, and electronically. In the year 2000, Richard was further challenged by Pastor Paul and Billy Graham to take this ministry fulltime; thus, started *ITW*"'s passionate efforts of training pastors and missionaries fulltime overseas, targeting Russia, China, and India. We incorporated (501-3c) as a ministry with the launch from our interactive Website, again, at the personal request of Billy Graham.

One of the great tragedies of the church today is that fewer and fewer people are reading the Bible. Fewer and fewer people are living the life of a disciple of Jesus Christ than ever before. As Christians living in America today, we tend to be more concerned with who is coming to our church and how many are coming, and less concerned with making disciples, which is our first and foremost call.

We believe that the lack of Bible study and Bible knowledge is one of the root causes of the problems that most Christians face, because without this knowledge, they are unable to make healthy and wise decisions. It is also one of the root problems that our *churches* face. Our churches are riddled with conflict and strife thereby pushing people away when we are called to be a light in darkness, salt to a flavorless world, and a haven of rest. Yet, we choose to ignore our call and rather place our focus upon our selfish needs and quests, when it needs to be upon the foot of the cross, who Christ is, and what He did for us as revealed in His Word.

Because of the aforementioned reasons, we have remained committed to Christ and His call at *Into Thy Word Ministries*. We are committed to teaching people how to find the time for Him, how to be His disciples, and how to understand His Word. In so doing, we believe that the church will flourish in power and commitment for our Lord's glory! Then, we can be the light in darkness, the flavor, and the rest in the midst of life's harshness. We can be the people of God so we can do the work of God!

You can Partner with us by:

1. **PRAYING -** Both personally and professionally so the word gets out about why learning how to study the Bible is important. In Matthew 9:37, 38 Jesus said, *the harvest is plenteous, but the laborers are few*. We need dedicated missionaries to teach biblical exegetical methods to pastors overseas, and we need people to help with administration and fundraising. We have many other places of opportunity, too.

2 **GIVING** - We are missionaries, and *ITW* is a mission endeavor. We receive no salary while carrying out Christ's Great Commandment and Great Commission; however, this requires money. With few exceptions, most of us could give more for the Lord's work.

3 **HELPING** - We are always looking for people to help us with administration, fundraising, and translating our "Pastor Training Packs" into different languages. We are always looking for people to distribute them, too.

4 **PROMOTING** - We need people to spread the word about *Into Thy Word*, and how people can get more out of their Bible and receive free, quality discipleship tools.

I want to know Christ and the power of his resurrection and the fellowship of sharing in his sufferings, becoming like him in his death, and so, somehow, to attain to the resurrection from the dead. Philippians 3:10-11

If you feel that you could be a part of this plan, any gift that you give would be extremely appreciated. If you feel led to support us, you may give "online" or conventionally. A onetime gift or an ongoing monthly commitment of your choice is greatly needed. Your financial gift will be the tool that God uses to keep this vital ministry going all over the world, but it is your ongoing prayers that will give us the strength, protection, and encouragement we need to make an impact.

Please consider helping us spread the word about God's Word as we teach biblical principles as well as how people can get more out of their Bible and how they can grow in Christ through our ministry.

Need discipleship materials? Does your church have you dejected or confused? Do you need helpful insights to know how to lead biblically, or some encouragement to keep steady in the faith? We are here to help outfit you for the Christian life. Check out our website; we have over 700 articles of solid Bible curricula designed to help you grow in Him.

You may also see "About" on our Website for more information, how to contact us, our statement of faith, and how you can better understand His Word.

THANK YOU for your support!

Into Thy Word Ministries

Family of Websites

www.intothyword.org
www.withtheword.org
www.pastortraining.org
www.truespirituality.org
www.francisschaeffer.org
www.biblestudynotes.org
www.discipleshiptools.org
www.churchleadership.org
www.biblicaleschatology.org
www.acts29.org

All about Small Groups!

How to Start and Lead Small Groups in your Church with His Power and Purpose!

The Author, Richard Joseph Krejcir is the cofounder and Director of *Into Thy Word Ministries*, a missions and discipling ministry. He is the author of several books including *Into Thy Word*, *A Field Guide to Healthy Relationships* and *Net-Work*. He is also a pastor, teacher, researcher, and speaker. He is a graduate of Fuller Theological Seminary in Pasadena, California (M.Div.) and holds a Doctor of Philosophy in Practical Theology from London (Ph.D). He has garnered over 20 years of pastoral ministry experience, mostly in youth ministry, including serving as a Church Growth Consultant.

And we urge you, brothers and sisters, warn those who are idle and disruptive, encourage the disheartened, help the weak, be patient with everyone. Make sure that nobody pays back wrong for wrong, but always strive to do what is good for each other and for everyone else. 1 Thessalonians 5:14-16

ISBN-13: 978-1468111385

Into Thy Word Ministries
129 South Lotus Avenue
Pasadena, Ca 91107

info@intothyword.com
www.intothyword.org

The LORD bless you and keep you; the LORD make his face shine upon you and be gracious to you; the LORD turn his face toward you and give you peace. Numbers 6:24-26

50256378R00113

Made in the USA
Lexington, KY
09 March 2016